Fairness, equality, leadership and justice had been values instilled in prisoner 46664 from his earliest years among his Xhosa people. Nelson Mandela had been a leading figure in the struggle for change in the apartheid state of South Africa. That is why he was in one of the toughest prisons in the world. Robben Island's maximum security prison, built to house political prisoners, offered no escape route. The treatment was brutal and numbers came before names.

Yet, more than four decades after his imprisonment the name Mandela continues to be an inspiration in the on-going struggle to create a better world.

INSPIRATIONS SERIES

Series Editor: Rosemary Goring

An easy-to-read series of books
that introduce people of achievement
whose lives are inspirational.

Other titles in the series:

Robert Burns
Bob Dylan
The Williams Sisters

Further titles to follow in 2011

Nelson Mandela

Robben Island to Rainbow Nation

Marian Pallister

ARGYLL✠PUBLISHING

Argyll Publishing
Glendaruel
Argyll PA22 3AE
Scotland
www.argyllpublishing.com

**British Library
Cataloguing-in-
Publication Data.
A catalogue record for
this book is available
from the British
Library.**

The publisher
acknowledges subsidy
from the Scottish Arts
Council towards the
publication of this
volume.

Scottish
Arts Council

ISBN 978 1 906134 53 5

Printing: JF Print Ltd,
Somerset

To my beautiful
sons, Jackson
and Charles,
who deserve an
equal place in a
fair society
in their own
country, Zambia.

Contents

Introduction

Johannesburg, South Africa, June 16th, 1976.
Twelve-year-old Hector Pieterson is shot in Vilakazi Street, Soweto. His schoolmate Mbuyisa Makhubo picks him up and runs with him towards the nearest clinic. Hector's sister Antoinette tries to keep up, crying all the way. All around them, bullets fly from police guns.

Was young Hector the member of a gang? A juvenile drug pusher? Had he and his mates just stabbed someone? Had they got hold of a gun and tried their hands at armed robbery?

No. Hector was just a schoolboy like all the rest who had joined a peaceful campaign march that morning. He was one of around 5,000 kids aged between 10 and 20 gathered in Vilakazi Street. They were going to march from their school to Orlando Stadium. A total of 15,000 students headed for the stadium on June 16, smartly dressed in their school uniforms despite the dust, despite the lack of washing facilities and electricity in their township homes in Johannesburg.

The campaign was against the government's order that black African children should learn half of their lessons in Afrikaans.

This was the language of the ruling minority white population and forcing black children to use it for their studies was going to disadvantage thousands. As the young people walked peacefully towards the stadium, the police opened fire. Hector, a bright, lively 12-year-old, took a bullet.

Robben Island, June 16th, 1976. *More than 1,400 kilometres from Soweto, the tragic news about the police action reaches men who have been smashing rocks with hammers for 12 years. Their sentence of hard labour is for their part in the African National Congress struggle against apartheid.*

Apartheid is the ugly word that describes the even uglier system of racial segregation put into operation by the Afrikaner National Party of South Africa from 1948.

Prisoner 46664 hears what has happened. Through the prison grapevine he learns that the final death toll in Soweto is 29 dead and 250 injured. He hears that the massacre has ignited support throughout South Africa for the anti-apartheid battle.

He says later: 'Information kept on coming through the prison walls about what was going on. . . the government actually produced one of the most rebellious generations of African youth. They were very militant; they were very brave. And there is nothing as encouraging to a political prisoner than to know that the ideas for which you are suffering will never die.'

Most of those who lose their lives on June 16th in Soweto are under 23 years old. By the end of the year, around 575 people will have died – 451 at the hands of the police. Many of the 3,980 injured are shot in the back and left crippled or maimed. Almost 6,000 people will have been arrested in the poor black townships by the time 1976 comes to a close.

Soweto, June 16th, 1976. *Press photographer Sam Nzima runs into the bullets to take a picture of Hector, who is dying in the arms of his fellow student. The police keep on shooting innocent teenagers.*

Nzima's photograph becomes an iconic image of the struggle in South Africa. It shocks the world. But the South African regime continues to repress its black citizens throughout the 1970s and 1980s.

Robben Island, June, 1976. *Prisoner 46664 and his fellow convicts are encouraged by Hector's tragic death to go on directing the struggle for human rights from within the prison walls. Number 46664 is determined to halt the injustices carried out against children like Hector and the adults who are discriminated against in every facet of their lives under the South African apartheid policy.*

In doing so, he becomes an inspiration to people around the world who believe in justice and freedom. His persistence ensures that young people like Hector Pieterson will have an equal place in a fair society.

Marian Pallister
January 2010

1. What's in a Name?

THIS BOOK is about Prisoner 46664, not Hector – although Hector's life deserves to be celebrated for the role he played in the struggle for human rights. There is a museum dedicated to him in Soweto that chronicles the dreadful day of his death and the lives of those who tried to change things in South Africa.

Prisoner 46664 had been a leading figure in that struggle for change. That is why he was in one of the toughest prisons in the world – Robben Island's maximum security prison, built in the 1960s to house political prisoners and soon known as 'the hell-hole of apartheid'. Situated almost four miles off the South African mainland at Cape Town, it offered no escape route. The treatment was brutal and numbers came before names.

The psychology of giving a prisoner a number is that it takes away identity, personality, self-worth – the very will to live. A life designated by a number has little significance.

The South African government that gave out this number in 1964 would have preferred that the judges had simply snuffed out this troublesome campaigner – had given him the death sentence instead of life imprisonment. They hoped that 46664 would be forgotten.

Instead, more than four decades after his imprisonment he continues to be an inspiration in the ongoing struggle to create a fairer world.

We know 46664 better as Nelson Mandela.

But even this is not his own name, and to understand why, we need to look at what was going on in South Africa in the 20th century.

Thanks to Nelson Mandela and those who fought alongside him for freedom, today's South Africa is a 'rainbow nation' – a country where black, brown and white are equal in the eyes of the law. That wasn't the way life was when Mandela was growing up: proud black peoples for whom the tip of the African continent had been home for millennia were reduced to serving the minority white population.

Mandela was born into the Xhosa tribe on July 18, 1918, and of course, he was given a Xhosa name, Rolihlahla. According to Mandela himself, this means 'pulling on the branch of a tree', but the colloquial meaning is 'troublemaker'. A few decades later, the white members of the South African government who had any knowledge of the Xhosa language would no doubt have agreed with both the formal and informal translations.

At the age of seven, Rolihlahala was sent to school. For the first time, he wore trousers, a cut down pair of his father's tied at the waist with string. He set out with a mixture of pride and apprehension. No child is totally confident on that first day in school.

Just to add to the confusion of the first-day experience, his teacher Miss Mdingane gave the bemused little boy a new name. He was to have a British education and a British name. It was randomly chosen and never explained to him why from that moment, Nelson was to be his 'official' name.

Many things were not explained to the black people of South Africa during much of the 20th century. Instead they were told to work here, live there, to carry documents proving that they had the right to be out on the street doing their shopping or speaking to a friend. Husbands and wives were separated. Children and young people were only allowed to use certain schools and colleges. A white man could tell a black man to run an errand for him in the street – and to make him walk in the road rather than on the pavement. Black people couldn't use the same transport as white people, go into the same cafés, or even attend the same sports events.

Many people are keen to point out that Nelson Mandela was born into a royal household, as if this alone was the reason for his ability to lead the struggle for justice in his country. If the image you have of 'royal' is the British monarchy, then you will be thinking of privilege, wealth, palaces, fancy clothes and crowns.

Although Nelson Mandela's family was given deep respect, you have probably guessed from the story of the cut-down trousers and the details about what black people were allowed and not allowed to do, that the House of Thembu had little in common with the House of Windsor.

The Thembu royal family governed the black people of the Transkei area of South Africa, a region bordering the Indian Ocean in the south east of this most southern state in the African continent. The family may once have been a driving force in this territory but by the time Nelson Mandela was born, it had little real influence in a national sense and the 'royal family' was answerable to local white magistrates and governors.

How had this come about? How was it that a member of a ruling family had to start school in his dad's trousers with the legs chopped off? Perhaps we need to look further back than just the 20th century – we have to do a bit of time travel back to the 15th century when things began to change for the indigenous peoples of southern Africa.

The Portuguese first landed there in 1488 and the British and the Dutch (known as Boers) started to arrive in numbers from the 1600s. The land, of course, was the home of many black tribes, each with its own ruling family. Traditionally, some were hunters and some were farmers, although their warriors also had a proud history.

What's in a Name?

What made Europeans – French Huguenots, British, Dutch and Germans – take what was then a dangerous journey of many months by sea to the other end of the earth?

The teacher in the movie *Sarafina* (about the 1976 uprising) makes a joke about the Cape having been nothing more than a filling station for Europeans on their way to the Far East, and that's a fair description of the situation in the 15th century.

But one of the very attractive things about this area for Europeans was the climate: it can grow many different crops, from oranges and grapes through wheat and maize to cotton, sugar and tobacco. People started to settle round the 'filling station' and they took the land from the local people to create their own farms. Their new lives were good.

There were other very attractive and lucrative things that lured people to this part of the world – diamonds, gold, coal, bauxite and many other valuable minerals. This was territory worth fighting over, and while the Zulu and Xhosa peoples were involved in some of the battles, by the 19th century the modern weaponry of the white people turned this into an on-going engagement between two groups of Europeans, the Dutch and the British.

Eventually, four states were created: the independent Boer Republics of the Transvaal and Orange Free State, and the British colonies of the Cape and Natal. By the late 19th century, the rivalry came to a head and led to the two Boer Wars. At the end of the second of these, which lasted from 1899 to 1902, the British had gained control.

In May 1910, the four states became the Union of South Africa, part of the British Empire but self-governing. The Union's constitution kept all political power in the hands of the white population: millions of black people were to have no say in how their country was run.

Two years later, a very important organisation was formed, the African National Congress (ANC), which aimed to give the majority black population a voice. Its quest was to be a long and difficult one, and it was into this unequal society that Rolihlahla Mandela was born.

2. The Family

ROLIHLAHLA'S father, owner of those chopped-off trousers, was called Gadla Henry Mphakanyiswa and he was a chief among the Thembu people, who are part of the bigger Xhosa nation. The Xhosa are the people whose language contains clicks that sound very exciting but make names and places difficult for non-Xhosa to pronounce properly. Try listening to Xhosa songs and raps on YouTube and you'll hear what I mean.

There is a clan system among the Xhosa and Rolihlahla's clan is the Madiba. 'Madiba' is a respectful name by which Nelson Mandela is also known.

But these were names for the future.

The Transkei is the area running down the eastern side of South Africa, next to the coast. That's where Rolihlahla was born, and at the time there was a Xhosa population of around 3.5 million living in Transkei alongside a very small number of Basothos and whites. The whites were the rulers and although Rolihlahla's father was confirmed as a chief by the king of the Thembu, under colonial rule the position was disrespected. When Rolihlahla's father had a dispute with the local white magistrate, his wage and land were stripped from him, leaving him so poor he couldn't dress his son properly for his first day at school.

Gadla Henry Mphakanyiswa's role within the Thembu royal family was to be adviser to the tribal rulers and it was assumed his son would follow in his footsteps. The Thembu lived in a polygamous society in which men were allowed as many wives as they could afford. Rolihlahla was the son of this respected man's third wife, Nosekeni, and lived with her in her own personal *kraal*, or collection of native huts, in Mvezo – a village in the district of Umtata, capital of the Transkei. There were four wives and thirteen children, living several miles apart in their own *kraals*. The marriages had, of course, taken place long before the unfortunate business with the magistrate.

Rolihlahla was the youngest of Gadla's four sons and the eldest of his mother's children. When his father stood up to the white magistrate and lost the wealth he had enjoyed, his mother had to move to a smaller village, Qunu, to bring up her family with the help of relatives.

Her son could remember nothing of the early better life, but revelled in growing up in a rural area, looking after sheep and calves and running free with his friends in the beautiful Transkei landscape.

His mother had three huts – one for sleeping, one for cooking and one where food was stored. Just as you will find in any southern African country today in traditional houses made from mud with a grass roof, there was no western-style furniture and the family slept on straw mats.

Rolihlahla went fishing with a piece of string and a hook made from barbed wire. He learned traditional stick fighting skills, parrying blows in a stylised fashion used for centuries by Xhosa warriors.

School was not on the agenda for most of his friends but his mother was friendly with a Methodist minister who suggested the boy should be educated. She approached his father, who not only gave his blessing but got out the knife to cut those trousers down to size. With a piece of string pulling in the grown-up waist to fit a seven-year-old, Rolihlahla was ready to become a student – and Nelson Mandela.

3. Lessons in Life

LIFE for black South African adults in the early 1920s may have been difficult – the women kept homes going in rural areas while men went off to Johannesburg to work in terrible conditions in the gold mines and other heavy industries – but for a child who came into little contact with prejudiced white people and who had the freedom to play under blue African skies, it was approaching perfect.

Young Nelson's idyllic childhood was cut short, however, when his father died of a chest infection during a visit to his mother's *kraal*.

He was then delivered up to Mqhekezweni where Chief Jongintaba Dalindyebo, acting regent of the Thembu people, had his royal residence. Mqhekezweni wasn't exactly a big city, but the Chief drove a Ford car and lived in a group of blindingly white-washed buildings. Nine-year-old Nelson was left in the Chief's care by his mother, who had to return home to her village. Jongintaba's offer to act as the boy's guardian could not be refused, whatever his mother might have preferred. Nelson was to see little of her in the years to come.

Instead, he lived in what was known as the 'Great Place'. He went to a one-roomed school to study

English, Xhosa, history and geography. This was a privilege in itself, because fewer than half of all African children attended school

People in Mqhekezweni wore western clothes and the Chief made sure Nelson was smartly dressed. He shared his life with Justice and Nomafu, the Chief's son and daughter, and occasionally with the Chief's eldest son, Sabata, who was heir to the throne.

In this setting, a very serious young Nelson acquired yet another name, the teasing 'Tatomkhulu' or 'Grandpa'. While Justice was away at secondary school, Tatomkhulu took great pride in ironing the Regent's western-style suits. Perhaps this was when Nelson began to form his own dress sense, which in later life would mark him out as a man of elegance and style.

It is almost certainly when he began to understand about fairness, equality, leadership and justice. Some of these grand concepts came from the Methodist church that he attended regularly; and some from witnessing his guardian in action.

The tribal councils held by Jongintaba involved a number of chiefs and village headmen. Although Jongintaba was the one who formally welcomed these men, it was they who discussed the issues that had been brought before the council. The talk might go on for hours and everyone would have his say without interruption until an agreement could be reached. If there was no agreement, a decision would be taken at a later time. The summing up by the Regent helped people reach a consensus.

Mandela has explained that majority rule was not part of this tribal culture and that in his own leadership, he always tried to listen to all points of view before giving an opinion. This method of government was what he witnessed during those tribal councils, when as a child he crept in to hear what was going on.

The councils were also a place where he could listen to the history of his own people, rather than the history of the invasive nations who had taken over his country. He could take a pride in knowing who his ancestors were, how they lived and what they achieved. The culture of his kinsmen – their ceremonies, dances, songs and stories – was in his blood.

One of his proudest moments was sharing the ceremonial circumcision that marked his transition from child to man. A group of teenagers prepared for this ritual together in a sacred place. They spent days together with tribal elders and then had to show their bravery by not flinching when the circumcision itself was performed. In the days after the ceremony, the young men continued to stay together in the huts built for the occasion, their wounds cared for by the elders. Then, the huts were burned and they returned to their homes to celebrate their coming of age.

He took home from this ritual yet another name –

Dalibhunga, his circumcision name, which means 'founder of the Bhunga', the traditional ruling organisation in the Transkei. For the Xhosa, this is Mandela's 'real' name.

When the white authorities brought all the African-run district councils together in one organisation called the United General Council of Transkei (locally known as the Bhunga), the 11-year-old Nelson Mandela had been present at the ceremony – a day of extravagant show by the white rulers. Although Nelson was fascinated by the customs and manners of the 'English gentlemen' that he saw at ceremonies like this and later learned about at secondary school, he was passionate about the importance of his own culture and was becoming increasingly aware that the ruling minority in his country gave it no respect.

Chief Meligqili, who gave a speech to the young men circumcised at the ceremony Nelson shared, must have hoped that his words would inspire at least one of them to set about changing the situation that black Africans found themselves in.

He told them that they were the pride of the Xhosa nation, but that like all black South Africans they were slaves in their own country, working in the mines in terrible conditions so that 'the white man can live a life of unparalleled prosperity'. He suggested that the abilities and intelligence of these young men would be wasted doing chores for the white man and that the celebratory gifts they were given that day held no value. The only gifts worth having – freedom and independence – could not be given.

These were words that no-one wanted to hear at a party and Nelson himself was annoyed because he had been taught to see the white man as benign rather than as tyrant. But he later admitted that Chief Meligqili had set him thinking.

4. Learning to be Black

NELSON Mandela got a pair of new boots to go to secondary school. They were his own, not hand-me-downs, and he was also given a send-off party when he left the Great Place for Clarkebury, the top school for black Africans.

He had so far not been exposed to the harsh laws and attitudes that shaped his countrymen's lives. Yes, his father had lost his position and income because of a minor disagreement with a white magistrate. Yes that controversial speech at his coming-of-age ceremony had been a bit of an eye-opener. But in rural Transkei the series of laws passed to limit the rights of black and mixed race people had so far not meant a lot to this boy of many names.

The Mines and Works Act of 1911 kept the best jobs for whites. The Black Land Act of 1913 reserved 92.7 per cent of the land in South Africa for whites. These laws pushed thousands of black people off the land they had farmed for generations and into the cities where they were only allowed to work as labourers in the mines and heavy industries. Racial segregation was strictly enforced.

Although Nelson Mandela was part of a ruling family whose power dated back to the 1400s, the secondary school he would go to would be for blacks only and English was the language he had to use in school. It was as if Xhosa was not a valid, written language. Yet the first newspaper for black Africans, *Umshumayeli* (Publisher of the News), had appeared as far back as 1837-41.

English was the official language of South Africa and those Africans who learned it were better able to go on to higher education and get better jobs. There was also Afrikaans, the language spoken by South Africans from a Dutch background, and it became the language of *apartheid*. Tough though the laws were when Mandela was going off to secondary school, they were not nearly as harsh as later.

Just as the Xhosa language books and newspapers were published by missionary organisations, so too were the majority of schools for black South Africans run by missionaries. Clarkebury had been founded in 1825 by Methodist missionaries on land in the district of Engcobo donated by the Thembu king Ngubengcuka, an ancestor of Mandela.

To celebrate Nelson's admission to Clarkebury, his guardian slaughtered a sheep to make a feast and then drove him in style across the Mbashe River in his Ford V8.

This school was, according to Mandela, 'the highest institution of learning for Africans in Thembuland'. He was being sent there to prepare him to carry on the family tradition of counselling the Thembu rulers. He would learn from black and white teachers, including the Reverend Cecil Harris, governor of the school. This was his first close encounter with a white man and shaking Mr Harris's hand – at 16 years old his first handshake with a white person – merits a mention in his autobiography.

Despite all his high-born connections, Nelson was treated the same as every other student at Clarkebury and he saw he would have to compete on merit. Although this was not the same child who had swapped stick fighting and cattle herding for elementary school in Qunu, Mqhekezweni was not after all the cool location Nelson had come to believe. Here at Clarkebury he was seen as painfully uncool in his clumpy new boots that warned people of his arrival at 50 paces.

His English teacher, Gertrude Ntlabathi, had been the first black woman in South Africa to gain a BA. Students also admired Ben Mahlasela BA, because he saw himself as an equal with his boss, Reverend Harris, at a time when a black graduate was expected to show great respect to white people, even to those in lower positions.

Nelson had a girlfriend at Clarkebury – Mathona – but she was not able to go on with her studies because her family couldn't afford the fees. Through-out Africa, little has changed. In the 21st century, thousands of young black Africans don't complete school or can't afford to go to college and university.

Nelson claimed not to be particularly clever or

particularly good at sport but he achieved his diploma in two years instead of three so perhaps modesty was always one of the Mandela qualities.

From Clarkebury he went at the age of 19 to Healdtown, another Methodist mission school and in 1937 the biggest African school south of the Equator. Here the head teacher was Dr Arthur Wellington, always keen to remind his students that his ancestor the Duke of Wellington defeated Napoleon at Waterloo.

The influences may have been exclusively British (a portrait of King George VI looked down on the students in the dining hall) but life was very African. Hot sugar water and dry bread was breakfast, 'samp' – a porridge made of maize kernels – sour milk and beans was a typical lunch, and dinner was a similar meal that rarely included meat.

The day started at 6am, studies continued to 5pm, when there was a break for exercise and food, and then continued again from 7pm to 9pm. Lights went out at 9.30pm. Mandela's dormitory housed 40 young men and the students supported their housemaster, Reverend Mokitimi, in his efforts to improve the diet and conditions experienced by the students.

One of Mr Mokitimi's reforms worried Mandela, however. The housemaster wanted to bring female students into the dining hall for Sunday lunch and the idea horrified Mandela, who was a country boy at heart and still not skilled in using a knife and fork. This meant many hungry Sundays for him.

He enjoyed two new sports, however, which he continued to practise into old age. Long distance running and boxing both needed self-discipline and he enjoyed what he called the 'solitariness' of the running. Little did he know how solitary life would become for him in later years.

It was at Healdtown that he began to have to make leadership decisions and to put into practice his ideas of justice. It may not rate alongside running a national political organisation and definitely doesn't equate with being president, but he recalls one particular judgment he was pushed into.

On rainy nights, students hated leaving the dormitory to get to the outside toilets and they broke all the rules by peeing over the verandah into the bushes. As a prefect, it was Mandela's job to stop this happening, or to report the culprits. One night he had 15 names in his notebook and saw yet another student watering the garden below. When he went to nab this latest culprit, he discovered it was a fellow prefect.

Mandela applied his legal and philosophical studies to his dilemma. If the prefect didn't obey the rules, how could anyone else be expected to? But one prefect wasn't supposed to report another. How unfair would it be to report the other 15 and not this one? Mandela decided to report no-one, and his long list was torn up.

5. Important to be Black

THERE are celebrities in every nation and every generation, and the Xhosa in the late 1930s were no exception. Krune Mqhayi was a famous poet, praise singer and oral historian. He trained as a teacher, worked as a journalist, was employed to improve the written language of the Xhosa, and was also a novelist. When he was invited to speak to students at Healdtown, nobody was going to miss the action.

There was something symbolic about Mqhayi's entrance on stage through the door only ever used by Dr Wellington – not only a black man coming through the exclusively white man's entrance but a black man wearing dramatic traditional dress. Mqhayi was dressed in a leopard skin *kaross* or cloak and matching headdress.

Mandela remembers him being disappointingly hesitant after this grand entrance – until he started to talk about the black-white divide in South Africa. Like the chief who had spoken at his circumcision ceremony, Samuel Edward Krune Mqhayi did not mince his words or offer the kind of respect to the white man that Mandela had been conditioned to give. Dr Wellington had been portrayed as the benefactor of all these students. Now Mqhayi was telling them,

'We cannot allow these foreigners who do not care for our culture to take over our nation.' He predicted that the 'forces of African society' would one day be victorious over the 'interloper'.

This was a bold speech and it was an influential one. The poem he then recited was even more so, ending as it did with him likening the proud and powerful Xhosa to the Morning Star. It had the students on their feet, cheering. Mandela said: 'I did not want ever to stop applauding.'

Mandela was gradually moving away from tribalism towards a feeling of unity with all Africans, but this poet's words confirmed in him his pride in being Xhosa.

Perhaps the most important idea that was emerging from his time at school was the realisation that all black South Africans were being crushed by the system; that although he was privileged to have been to school and looked like becoming the first in his clan to achieve a university degree, he was not free to choose his future in the same way that a young white South African could.

There was only one residential centre of higher education in South Africa for blacks. Scottish missionaries had founded University College at Fort Hare in 1916. There were just 150 students – no surprise when you think how few black South African children were attending even primary school, let alone having the opportunity to get into a university.

Mandela has explained that the missionary schools were less racist than those run by the South African government, which was often unwilling to build any schools at all for the black population.

One of the important figures at Fort Hare was Professor Davidson Don Tengo Jabavu, the first black professor at the University of Fort Hare. He remained at the university for more than thirty years and also founded a black teachers' association, which worked for racial co-operation. He was president of the All-Africa Convention (AAC), an umbrella organisation that consisted of several organisations opposed to the segregation legislations passed by the government in 1936.

Such a man had the charisma to impress blacks and whites alike and must surely have been influential in forming Mandela's view of what was happening to his country.

But Mandela was still following a conventional route, planning to be an interpreter or a clerk in the Native Affairs Department. These were civil service jobs and about as high as a black African could aspire to at the time. Being an interpreter to a rural magistrate was seen as an important position. He studied English, anthropology, politics, native administration and Roman Dutch Law. In his second year, he took a new interpreting course that had just been introduced at Fort Hare.

A third year student who was a family member,

K.D. Matanzima, advised him to study law so that he could be a counsellor to Sabata, his future tribal ruler. It was only later that he took this advice.

In the meantime, Mandela was being the universal student, taking part in new sports, joining the drama club, and learning to ballroom dance. He found he could overcome a lack of ability through 'diligence and discipline' – in other words, he discovered that if he put in the effort, whether at cross-country running or Roman Dutch Law, he came out on top while people with more ability than him but less self-discipline didn't do so well.

He was no saint, although he was a member of the Students' Christian Association. A group from the SCA used to go into the town of Alice on Sundays for a meal. As blacks couldn't eat in white-run restaurants, they had to go round to the back door and negotiate with the kitchen.

In one of the nearby villages, there was a place where blacks were allowed to go, although it was off-limits for Fort Hare students. It was an African dance hall called Ntselamanzi and, dressed in their suits, a group of SCA members invaded the place. An elegant young Mandela asked a young woman to dance and was showing off his newly-learned dance steps – until he asked his partner's name. She turned out to be the wife of a highly respected African leader who at that moment was chatting on the other side of the dance floor to one of Mandela's professors.

He politely led his partner off the dance floor and slunk off. The professor never mentioned the incident or the rules that Mandela had broken, presumably because he knew that off the dance floor, Mandela was a hard worker.

In many areas of life, the Fort Hare experience presented a steep learning curve for Mandela. There were many firsts – wearing pyjamas, using a tooth-brush and toothpaste, flushing toilets and hot showers among them. For Africans of his generation, beautiful white teeth were achieved with ash and toothpicks.

He was still quite naive about the political state of play in South Africa. By now, World War II was raging in Europe. The Fascism against which the Allied Forces were fighting had some distant echoes in South Africa. In the late 1930s, Prime Minister J.B. Hertzog had been all for taking a neutral stance. Deputy Prime Minister Jan Smuts, on the other hand, wanted South Africa to declare war on the Germans. Mandela was impressed by the fact that Smuts was a co-founder of the League of Nations – a forerunner of today's United Nations. This action on the world stage seemed to blind the young Mandela to Smuts' and Hertzog's actions at home, which had taken away votes from the few remaining Africans entitled to access to the ballot box.

When Smuts came to speak to students at Fort Hare, everyone agreed that South Africa should go to war against Germany. But a fellow student, Nyathi

Khongisa, raised the issue of Smuts' racism and warned that Germany and Britain might be enemies in Europe, but their descendants in South Africa would unite against 'the black threat'.

Mandela learned that Khongisa was a member of the African National Congress and admits in his autobiography that at university, he knew little of this organisation that had been founded six years before he was born to seek equality for Africans in South Africa.

By his second year at Fort Hare, he was beginning to learn more about the ANC through his friend Paul Mahabane, whose father was a leading figure in the organisation.

During his presidency of the ANC in the 1920s, Rev Z.R. Mahabane claimed that Africans were treated as children rather than adult citizens with full rights to self-determination, ownership of land, and equality under the law without discrimination on grounds of race, class or creed. This challenge was embodied in the 1923 ANC Bill of Rights, a document that remains relevant to all citizens of the world in the 21st century.

Mandela wasn't alone in thinking that his friend's father was a full-blown rebel and holidaying with Paul, he found that rebellion ran in the family. In Umtata, capital of the Transkei, a white magistrate stopped Paul and asked him to run and buy him stamps. Paul refused, argued with the magistrate and stood his ground when the magistrate became angry – his was the kind of request white men made of black people every day of the week and he expected the errand to be carried out with respect.

This was a revelation to Mandela. He admits that while he respected Paul for his reaction to the request, he wasn't yet ready to follow his example.

Things were beginning to stack up in his mind, however. The speeches, the actions, the situations he was increasingly being exposed to, raised his awareness of why bodies like the ANC existed – it wasn't a simple world after all. For him and his fellow blacks, life was hemmed in by legal restrictions and racist attitudes.

These restrictions and attitudes were already shaping the lives of other young men in different parts of South Africa. Although they had not yet met, their futures would be entwined with Mandela's.

Govan Mbeki, who would one day stand trial for his life alongside Nelson Mandela, stayed with his family in a black area of Johannesburg. Every weekend the whole community lived in fear when squads of police descended on the district, sealed off the escape routes and beat up the men, demanding their passes. No black African could move without a pass – a sort of complicated identity card – and those who couldn't produce one were arrested and slammed in jail.

Elias Motsoaledi, another who would stand trial

with Mandela, grew up in the Sekukuniland Reserve, one of the designated places where Africans were allowed to live. His family lived on four acres of ground, scraping a living from what could be grown there. Outside the reserve, thousands of acres of land owned by white farmers lay unused.

With a university degree under his belt, could Mandela's future be any easier than that of his peers? He certainly believed it could, and was already making plans to give his mother a better life. Plans, however, don't always work out.

6. Defying Authority

IT IS A LESSON that is hard to learn, but it is always best to know that taking a stand and sticking to your principles doesn't always have immediate rewards.

On the eve of the end of his second year, Mandela was involved in a student campaign for better conditions at Fort Hare. The principal, Dr Kerr, manipulated the outcome of a boycott on voting and Mandela found himself faced with withdrawing his resignation from a committee that had been elected by an unrepresentative minority – or being expelled. After a troubled night of indecision, he decided to stick to his guns. Dr Kerr gave him some space to come back from the brink by offering him the chance to return to Fort Hare for his final year, but only if he agreed to join the student representative council.

He thought he had been right to take a stand but when he returned home, his uncle didn't agree and ordered him to return to Fort Hare after the holiday.

In the meantime, a bigger problem faced Mandela and his cousin Justice. The Regent wasn't just issuing orders about university that holiday – he also wanted to marry off the two young men. He explained that he didn't want to die without settling his affairs and that he had arranged marriages for them both that were to take place immediately.

Mandela had had girlfriends, believed in love matches, and was prepared to rebel against this traditional way of going about things. Justice was also against his father's plan and the pair decided to run away to Johannesburg.

It wasn't the responsible way to deal with the situation, but it seemed like a good idea at the time. The Regent was to be away for a week attending the Bungha and so the lads packed a bag, raised cash by selling one of the Regent's farm animals, hired a car and headed for the station. The Regent knew they were up to something and had told the stationmaster not to sell them tickets, so they had to take the hire car on to the next station and get a train there.

They had, of course, to show their pass books, which showed where they lived, who their chief was and whether they had paid the poll tax levied only on black Africans. Without passes, as Govan Mbeki knew from those weekend raids in Johannesburg, they could be arrested, fined or jailed. Justice and Nelson had acceptable passes but not the permits any African needed to cross from one district to another.

They compounded their stupidity by lying to a relative to get the travel permits. The relative put a call in to check that it was in order – and got an earful from the Regent, who demanded that they be arrested. Nelson's small knowledge of the law persuaded this official not to arrest them, but they were turned out of his office in disgrace.

Undeterred, the two young men continued, illegally, to Johannesburg where their eyes were out on stalks at the size and grandeur of the city. At Crown Mines they blagged their way into employment and the university student found himself working as a night watchman.

The disagreement with Fort Hare's principal had threatened his university career. Running away from an arranged marriage without seeking to discuss the options seemed to have slammed the door on a degree.

7. The First Brush with the Law

CROWN MINES was the biggest in Johannesburg and had been in operation since the 1880s. It was a dirty, stinking, brutal place and the hostels in which the miners lived matched their working conditions. The gold ore was deep underground but cheap black labour allowed it to be very profitable for the white owners.

When Justice's father found out where the runaways were he used his influence to get them thrown out of their jobs. There were a few difficult days but Mandela tracked down some relatives and landed on his feet.

A young black estate agent called Walter Sisulu introduced him to a white lawyer, Lazar Sidelsky. Sidelsky was persuaded to take Mandela on as a trainee. The young man who had set such store by his university education and had been so distressed by his expulsion from university was now discovering that people who were successful in Johannesburg didn't all have degrees – they just worked the system.

He did eventually complete his own studies by correspondence course through the University of South Africa but an education of a different kind was now to begin.

Mandela learned that there were kind and generous liberal whites like Sidelsky, and prejudiced whites like the office girls who made sure Africans drank from their own cups at tea breaks and told Mandela to run and buy shampoo when a client was in the room because they did not like it to be known that they were working for a black man. Mandela was generous enough to run the errand.

He learned that there were deeply thoughtful political men like Walter Sisulu, who was involved with the African National Congress, and Nat Bregman, a Communist who demonstrated his beliefs by sharing a sandwich equally with Mandela.

He started to hang out with Sisulu and Bregman at political meetings and parties where politics were discussed avidly by a mix of young black, white and brown guests. In part, these discussions began to influence Mandela's thinking.

But there were other factors forming his ideas about his country. Living conditions in Alexandra, a black area of Johannesburg, were very different from anything Mandela had ever experienced. Poverty in the countryside can be gentler than poverty in a city, and Alexandra could only be described as a rough, tough slum.

There were no roads, no electricity, and women and children had to go with containers to the nearest outdoor tap to carry water for cooking and washing. The place stank with rubbish and because cooking was done outside on coal fires lit in old oil drums with holes punched into them, the air was always smoky. Children ran about in scraps of ragged clothing, escaping from their makeshift homes that were enterprisingly cobbled together from bits of corrugated iron, wooden planks and mealie meal bags.

It was noisy and scary. At night, Mandela often heard gunshots and screams. He quickly learned to avoid the gang members who stalked Alexandra carrying blades. Too many people were drunk on the beer brewed from maize and sugar in the back yards of illegal drinking dens. And then there were the police raids that were part of daily life – white officers pushing around black citizens, demanding their passes, looking for illegal alcohol, beating people up on the slightest excuse.

It sounds like the worst place in the world to live, but because it was one of the few places where black people ran their own lives it attracted thousands of Africans of every tribal background. This melting pot created a unity among black Africans that worried the minority white government.

Mandela was to admit: 'I learned more about poverty in that first year [in Johannesburg] than I did in all my childhood in Qunu.' He had to live on £2 a week, paying rent, transport, food, candles and fees for his University of South Africa correspondence course. The candles were so he could study in the evenings. He couldn't afford to buy clothes, often went hungry, and at the end of the week before he got his pay packet, he had to walk the six miles to work because he didn't have the fare for the 'natives-only' bus.

There were friends from school who occasionally fed him, friends who became girlfriends, and the family he rented his room from made sure he at least ate on Sundays. He survived, and he grew up.

Although his newly found self-confidence meant he no longer needed to call on his family connections for support, those connections did mean the door was open to many important people. When he decided to move into the miners' hostel to save money, he was around in the office when tribal leaders came to town. He met and talked with most of them, including the queen regent of Basutoland, an area now known as Lesotho. She was kind enough to talk to him, but criticised his lack of different tribal languages. How was he to be a successful lawyer and help his people if he didn't speak their languages, she wanted to know?

He took the point to heart. His experiences in Johannesburg were giving him an insight into the lives of the majority of black South Africans. He saw that he had to use his education to make changes – and as the queen regent of Basutoland made clear to him, he had to continue his education so that he could communicate with everyone.

With a BA under his belt, he was now being

introduced to politics in a big way by Gaur Radebe, one of his colleagues in Sidelsky's office, and by Walter Sisulu. Wisely, he didn't jump straight into the deep end of these political waters.

First, he went to meetings and listened. He heard debates about everything from bus fares to the way the government was run.

Then he went on a protest march. Just as young Hector Pieterson would three decades later, a youthful Nelson Mandela joined with 10,000 others to march against a rise in the bus fares from four pence to five. He had walked the walk, now he could add his voice to those affected by such a drastic demand on their meagre weekly budget.

The protest went on for nine days. No-one travelled in the buses and the size of the march made it clear how many were willing to back the boycott. At the end of the nine days, the bus company agreed to continue at the old fare. Result!

Mandela explained what it felt like to switch from observer to participant. Yes, it was inspiring to march in protest but, he said, 'I was also impressed by the boycott's effectiveness.'

His boss, Mr Sidelsky, warned him that politics could lead nowhere except to trouble, bankruptcy, family break-up and jail. This kindly white man could hardly have known how very true his predictions would be. They certainly shook Mandela – but as he points out in his autobiography, while at university, the teachers avoided talking about racial oppression and the lack of opportunities for Africans. Even the laws and regulations that tied the black man in knots and made life impossible were taboo subjects.

'But in my life in Johannesburg, I confronted these things every day.' He adds: 'No-one had ever suggested to me how to go about removing the evils of racial prejudice, and I had to learn by trial and error.'

People sometime equate prejudice with ignorance. Mandela found that even the most highly educated in the land were capable of making their feelings about blacks very clear – like the fellow student at law school (where Mandela was the only African) who carefully picked up all his belongings when Mandela sat in a seat next to him at a lecture. With a great deal of show, the student moved to another seat.

But at the University of Witwatersrand, where he began his law studies, he also met very liberal whites who would play very important roles in the struggle for equality in South Africa.

Joe Slovo and Ruth First (who became Joe's wife), George Bizos and Bram Fischer became names almost as well known as Nelson Mandela's as the movement grew to rid the country of *apartheid*.

This was also a time when Mandela became involved with young people of Asian descent who were also affected by racial attitudes and laws in South

Africa. It was as a result of these new friendships that Mandela ended up in court, for the first but not the last time, with Bram Fischer defending him and his Indian friends.

They had all boarded a tram – something Indians but not Africans could do. The conductor told the Indians that their '*kaffir* friend' (an abusive term) couldn't ride on the tram. An argument about the insult followed and Mandela and his friends were arrested. Fischer, who was a member of a very important political Afrikaner family, got them acquitted.

All of this served to show Mandela that politics was not something you went into in middle age – it was for young people. Everyone at law school who was fired up and ready to sacrifice everything for the liberation struggle was of the same generation as him. He knew there could be no more sitting on the fence. If young Indians and Afrikaners were prepared to fight to bring equality to Africans, he had to be, too.

8. Taking a Stand

IT WAS, of course, wise to have taken his time to get into politics. He had to see things from other people's points of view. Although he had grown up in a world where it was the norm to have an 'Africans Only' label put on everything from a ride in a bus to a place in the maternity hospital, from school to work, he had been lucky. As a member of an important African family, he went to school and had a place at university. His friends and connections had got him a job in a firm that was prepared to send him on to study still further.

Yes, he had to live in an 'Africans Only' area, was arrested for riding on a tram from which Africans were excluded, and had experienced the snubs dished out routinely by prejudiced white people.

But it was seeing how badly the laws and regulations affected each and every member of his race in South Africa that pushed him over the edge and into active politics. Around the world, countries were signing up to new, liberal-thinking charters that demanded human rights for all. The Atlantic Charter signed in Europe in 1941 inspired the ANC to draw up its own charter calling for full citizenship for all Africans.

Hanging out at Walter Sisulu's place – a very

welcoming home – brought Mandela into contact with some very exciting and interesting Africans. Anton Lembede was proud of the colour of his skin and was possibly the first person that Mandela had heard say that black was beautiful. Lembede condemned what he saw as an African inferiority complex. He demanded self-reliance and self-determination and Mandela was right to see him as a future leader.

Mandela realised that he had been living in awe of the colonial past. Now he understood that instead of trying to be 'British' he had to fight to allow his countrymen to be 'African'.

The older generation of Africans who to date had led the ANC were far too polite in seeking change. Now, under the leadership of Anton Lembede, a group of young guys including William Nkomo, Walter Sisulu, Oliver Tambo, Ashby Mda and Nelson Mandela set out to change things. These young men were faced with what seemed like an impossible task, but with a group of just 60 members, they began to turn the ANC into a mass movement that would fight for rural farmers, illiterate miners, and struggling young professionals like themselves.

In September 1944, while World War II was still being fought in Europe and the Far East, these young men founded the African National Congress Youth League (ANCYL). By 1947 Mandela had been elected as secretary. Meanwhile, Lembede, Mda and Tambo were elected onto the national executive committee of the ANC itself.

In time, Mandela and Oliver Tambo would become partners in a law firm that helped Africans fight the system. They would face queues of clients who had been arrested for all sorts of petty 'crimes' – being out on the street without a passbook, travelling on transport reserved for whites – as well as people with run-of-the-mill legal issues that most Africans could ill afford to sort out but for whom Mandela and Tambo were prepared to work.

These clients were victims – like all Africans – of laws passed by the white minority government over a long period of time.

From the time the ANC had been in existence, the restrictions had been multiplying. There was the 1913 Black Land Act, which took most of the land out of the hands of blacks. There was the 1923 Urban Areas Act that forced blacks to live in what quickly became slum areas. These areas were called 'native locations' and they were placed next to the major industries so that there was a supply of cheap labour. The 1926 Colour Bar Act banned Africans from working in skilled trades – if you were black, you couldn't be a plumber or an engineer. The Native Administration Act of 1927 had taken the power from the Paramount Chiefs and given it to the British Crown (in other words, civil servants in London ruled the lives of Africans and the traditional leaders were silenced). The 1936 Representation of Natives Act denied all Africans the vote.

At that time in many countries around the world,

the granting of a vote, or franchise, was based on certain conditions, such as gender. Many women still didn't have the vote (in France, for instance, the majority of women were not given the vote until 1947). Owning property was a condition in some countries. In most countries, voters had to be over 21 and in others, women had to be over 30. But in most places, governments were at least negotiating with campaigners and the extension of the franchise was on most governments' agendas. Nowhere but South Africa saw taking the vote away from the majority of the population as a reasonable piece of law making.

These years of oppression were what led up to the formation of the ANCYL and its manifesto declared: 'We believe that the national liberation of Africans will be achieved by Africans themselves.'

The oppression also led to a lot of unrest through-out South Africa. In 1946, 70,000 miners went on strike to get better pay for their fellow workers. The country's 400,000 miners earned just two shillings a day. The unions were asking for a living wage of ten shillings a day, family housing instead of the male-only hostels that split up families, and two weeks' holiday a year.

The bus strike had been successful, but that was staged against a commercial organisation that crumbled when it lost money. The miners' strike was unsuccessful. The men were fighting the government and the government was ruthless in arresting strike leaders and ordering police to deal brutally with protest marchers. Twelve miners died.

Mandela went from mine to mine, talking to the men and helping to organise what the union could do next, working with the union leader J.B. Marks.

The strike got nowhere and 52 men were prosecuted for sedition – in other words, the government accused them of inciting people to rebellion, of treason, charges that carried the death penalty. This was intended to crush any further protest against injustice, but the Indian community set a great example that Mandela was inspired to follow.

This came about when the Indian community was targeted by the government. They, too, were told where to live and where they could trade, and there were restrictions on their right to buy property.

For two years, thousands conducted a mass campaign of passive resistance. Indians of every class picketed and occupied land meant for whites. Over 2,000 volunteers were jailed and the leaders were sentenced to six months' hard labour.

The Youth League was impressed. The Indians had got their act together and their protest was highly organised. The ANC had never managed that. Mandela and the other Youth League leaders decided it was time they did.

Militant mass action rather than speeches and resolutions became the ANCYL's strategy. They knew the police would beat them up. They knew they would go to jail – maybe even die. But it was a strategy guaranteed to attract the attention of the outside world and the support of other countries was what black Africans desperately needed.

They got it: too many lives had been lost in the fight against Fascism during the 1930s and 1940s for a new Fascist state to be ignored. And that was how South Africa was seen when in 1948 the National Party (with an all-white vote, of course) won the general election. The National Party's main policy was *apartheid* – an Afrikaans word that on the page of the dictionary means nothing more sinister than 'separateness' but in practice classified citizens in racial groups (white, black, coloured and Indian). The law decided the separate areas where each of these groups was allowed to live and the law was now enforced by physically removing people from their homes. The new government also confirmed the segregation of health services, education and all other public services.

In the coming years the government denied blacks citizenship of South Africa and instead made them citizens of self-governing homelands based on tribal background. This was a cunning ploy that seemed to give people a voice but in fact took it away from them.

By 1949, the ANCYL had decided to use all the non-violent methods of resistance that they could – boycott, strikes, civil disobedience and non-cooperation. Mandela, along with Sisulu, Tambo and others, drew up this Programme of Action and the main ANC was also happy to accept it as its policy.

Mandela was one of the main authors of this programme. What he wanted was full citizenship for blacks and full representation in parliament. If you can't vote, you have no voice. Mandela wanted a voice for the voiceless people of his country.

That didn't just mean a vote for a member of parliament. After that experience of the miners' strike, Mandela understood how important it was for people to be allowed to be members of trades unions – and for the trades unions to have the right to negotiate with the bosses of both private companies and government-run operations.

He also put access to education, land rights and culture on the ANCYL agenda. He believed that all children should have free and compulsory education. But he knew that millions of his fellow countrymen had not had his opportunities and were often completely uneducated, so he wanted adults to have access to education too.

By this time, Lembede was dead. Mandela had driven him to hospital one night in July 1947 after he had complained of stomach pains. He didn't last the night. At the age of just 33, he left a big hole in the leadership of the ANCYL.

Peter Mda, who took over, wasn't such a wildcat as Lambede, but he had lots of influence. Like

Mandela, he knew it was white oppression that was the problem, not individual white people – but Mandela admitted that he wasn't happy about having white members of the Youth League and he certainly didn't want Communist members.

Mandela had been elected to the Executive Committee of the Transvaal ANC, and began to find out how many sacrifices had to be made if he was going to commit himself to fighting for the rights of his people. When his baby daughter died, he knew he didn't spend enough time at home to comfort his wife Evelyn.

But he was up against a political party that had slogans such as '*Die wit man moet altyd baas wees*' – 'The white man must always remain boss.' How degrading to have politicians stand up and use words like '*baasskap*' – meaning 'boss-ship' in the same way that the white man in Umtata had meant it when he told Mandela's friend to run an errand for him.

Mandela had to make choices: spend his time cosily at home at night with his family; or go out on the road to fight for change.

Young Nelson Mandela chose the fight. This was not because he didn't love his family, but because he hated apartheid, which he describes in his autobiography as 'a new term but an old idea'. The segregation that had been put in place informally for centuries was now, with the 1948 election result, to be enforced brutally by law.

Although the ANC hadn't thought the National Party would win the election, Oliver Tambo was happy with the result because he now knew whom he was fighting. It was pretty clear what kind of a government the country had voted for itself – a pro-Nazi criminal was pardoned within weeks of the National Party coming to power. Then the coloureds (mixed race people) had the vote taken from them. The Prohibition of Mixed Marriages Act followed, and then the Immorality Act – so it wasn't only illegal to marry someone of a different race, it was illegal to have sexual relationships between black and white.

And if you weren't sure what race you were, the government would decide for you. Then they would send you to live in the appropriate area set out for your race. Decisions of racial classification were made by policemen or civil servants based on made-up criteria such as the shape of someone's shoulders (seen from the back), how curly their hair was or the shape of their mouths. Families were split if it was decided one partner was coloured and another was black.

On a day-to-day basis, people could be 'banned'. This meant that they were not allowed to meet with friends, even in their own homes, and certainly not allowed to take part in political meetings. The political meetings, boycotts and strikes went ahead, however, sometimes with horrific consequences.

A general strike was planned for May 1, 1950. The Communist Party and the India Congress called the strike, demanding that the pass laws be abolished and discrimination brought to an end. Mandela didn't want the ANC to take part and had an argument about it with Ahmed Kathrada, the 21-year-old leader of the Transvaal Indian Youth Congress. Kathrada challenged him, saying there was African support for the strike. It was to be the first of many discussions the two would have. They were soon to find they were sharing not just their politics but their lives.

Of course, the government banned meetings and marches on the day of the strike, and although the protest march was peaceful and there was no provocation from the crowd, Mandela and Walter Sisulu went along to one of the marches and were terrified when police started shooting at them. Then they saw mounted police ride their horses into the crowd and smash into people with their batons. Mandela and Sisulu took shelter and heard bullets ricochet off the building. The death toll was 18 Africans. Many more were seriously injured.

The outcome of this mayhem was a range of new laws banning political parties and all sorts of other organisations. New powers let the government arrest any individual who opposed government policies. As a member of the ANC National Executive, Mandela knew what to expect.

The ANC held its own Day of Protest on June 26, 1950 and even though it was classed as nothing more than 'a moderate success', Mandela found it exhilarating to organise this kind of event.

9. The Fight vs. Family

THIS FIGHT for equality had become a young man's fight. The respected traditional leaders were given their place, but more and more it was members of the younger generation who were leading Africans against this repressive regime.

Perhaps this was because the young men were at the sharp end of the oppression. Remember, in Mandela's childhood in the countryside, he knew little of the bullying prejudice dished out by too many white South Africans. And the older generation still lived in the rural areas, while young people had to go off to the towns to scratch a living. And there in the towns, young families experienced the full force of the brutality of this Nazi-like society.

Even a man like Mandela, educated, working in the legal profession, studying to become an attorney, experienced the heavy hand of the state in his private life as well as in his political life. He had married a trainee nurse, Evelyn Mase, and in 1946 their son Madiba Thembekile was born. They were told where to live and the size of their house was dictated by the state.

The couple were given a new house with two rooms that cost 17s 6d a month in rent. It had a tin roof, cement floor and a bucket toilet outside. There was no electricity so they used paraffin lamps. The bed took up all the space in the second room.

This was identical to thousands upon thousands of workers' houses built in ugly rows. Mandela felt proud that he had a home of his own and proud that he had a son. But such allocations did not take account of Xhosa tradition that opens its doors to any family member. Just as Mandela himself had been given room in the homes of friends and relatives during his first years in Johannesburg, so Nelson and Evelyn gave a home to his sister Leabie and enrolled her in the nearby Orlando high school.

Sometimes there were semi-permanent guests that the Mandelas (or more probably, Nelson himself) gave refuge because they were in trouble. Once in 1946 that meant sheltering two church ministers along with the wife and children of one of them.

A second son was born to the Mandelas and given the very political name of Makgatho Lewanika. Mapogo Makgatho had been a president of the ANC who led a protest against Africans being barred from walking on the pavement in Pretoria. Lewanika was a Zambian chief. They were inspirational names – but they didn't make up for Mandela being an absent father. His five-year-old son Thembi, according to his wife, had asked 'Where does Daddy live?' when Daddy was away from home more than 18 hours out of the 24.

By the early 1950s, when Mandela had passed his driving test, 'Daddy' was away even more than ever, sometimes legally and sometimes illegally depending on the mood of the police at the time.

In 1952, he delivered a letter from the ANC to Dr Daniel Malan, leader of the Nationalists, demanding a repeal of the restrictions on blacks. If the government didn't agree, the ANC would take action. Malan replied that the white community were within their rights to preserve their own identity and if the ANC took action, the government would use its full powers against members.

A policy of civil disobedience was now the only route for the ANC. Mandela, who was put in charge of organising the campaign, spoke to the unions explaining there could be no violence whatsoever, whatever force the police or government troops used.

The Defiance Campaign was to start on 26th June and blacks would deliberately use whites-only toilets, train compartments, post office entrances and restaurants. They would stay in town after curfew. They would do this in groups and inform the police beforehand.

The next stage was to be a series of strikes.

Mandela drove around talking to groups 10,000 strong, each time emphasising unity between Africans, coloured and Indians. Respected community leaders dressed in old clothes in preparation for spending a night in jail. Protesters sang freedom songs as they were arrested.

It was a campaign that ran for six months and Mandela toured all around the country firing up groups who were to take part in different actions. The government was not happy with the success of the campaign because it united all of the racial groups that *apartheid* intended to divide. They tried to infiltrate the ranks of the ANC and sometimes succeeded, but on the other hand, there were many black policemen who secretly helped the campaign, risking their lives to do so.

Government forces raided the homes and offices of the protest leaders and took away what they hoped would be incriminating documents. Mandela's own office at the law firm H.M. Basner was also raided and Mandela was arrested on a charge that accused him of being a Communist.

He and 20 other leaders of the ANC, South African Indian Congress, ANC Youth League and Transvaal Indian Congress were tried in Johannesburg in September 1952, which sparked off more huge demonstrations that included white university students, schoolchildren, campaigners from Alexandra and people of every race. Shouts of '*Mayibuye Afrika*' (Let Africa come back) rang round the courtroom.

The case could have been a triumph for the protesters, but Dr J.S. Moroka, a figurehead in the ANC, chose to save his own skin and destroyed the image of solidarity. In December, all were found guilty of 'statutory Communism' and sentenced to nine months' hard labour. This jail sentence was suspended for two years, so none of the accused actually went to prison.

Despite the setbacks (and of course, as the campaigners knew would be the case, the laws were not repealed) this six months of action was a success because it established the ANC as a force to be reckoned with and membership was now 100,000.

Although 40 people were killed in unrelated riots (which the government tried to pin on the ANC), there had been no violence carried out by campaigners. Mandela recognised that the protest went on too long and that the organisers, including himself, were not yet professional enough.

But Mandela now saw himself as a freedom fighter and was proud to be one.

10. Defending the Masses

BY THE END of 1952, Mandela was the chief of four deputy presidents of the ANC, supporting the new president, Chief Albert Luthuli.

Unfortunately, he wasn't able to go to the ANC's national conference because he was one of 52 leaders banned from attending meetings or gatherings for six months. The government knew exactly what it was doing – the ban was slapped on Mandela just days before the conference was due to start. For the next six months he had to stay in Johannesburg.

You might think this would have been good for family life; that every cloud has a silver lining. But this was South Africa under an iron-fisted *apartheid* government. By 'meetings' and 'gatherings' the ban meant any get-together – including Mandela's little boy's birthday party. He couldn't talk to more than one person at a time.

Imagine how restrictive that must have been: if he talked to Evelyn, he couldn't allow his sister in the room at the same time or he would be arrested. And yes, the police did raid houses on a very regular basis to see if the bans were being followed.

These bans were put in place time after time over the next decade, leaving Mandela frustrated and living his life illegally most of the time. He called the effect of these bans 'psychological claustrophobia'.

Mandela could see that the next step after banning so many of the ANC leaders would be to ban the ANC itself, along with its allies. The National Executive commissioned him to draw up the Mandela Plan (known as the M-Plan) that would allow the organisation to operate underground. The ANC and its allies were to operate through small underground cells that could activate action in streets, districts and ultimately, country-wide.

He was also one of a number of lecturers who taught small groups in secret – discussing such issues as the way that blacks were oppressed as both a race and an economic class. Meetings of the leadership also took place in secret. This system had some success, but members and leaders were sure the government wouldn't take drastic action.

It did.

By this time, Mandela had become an attorney, thanks to Evelyn's financial support for his studies. He had left the office of H.M. Basner and got together with his friend Oliver Tambo to set up their own law firm in Chancellor House, Johannesburg, opposite the magistrates' court. There were other African lawyers, of course, but theirs was the only firm of African lawyers and so they were the first choice for African clients.

The list of 'crimes' Africans could commit under

the Nationalist government was growing longer. You could be prosecuted for being unemployed or employed in the wrong place. You could be jailed for being homeless. You could be evicted from land your family had farmed for generations. You could be evicted from your home because the area was suddenly reclassified as a whites-only area (and then, of course, being homeless you could be jailed).

Whether you had been fingered for drinking at a whites-only water fountain, or for being out after 11pm, or persecuted because the government had moved the residential or employment goalposts, Mandela and Tambo were Africans who understood and would fight your corner.

Of course, Mandela and Tambo themselves faced difficulties. Some white witnesses were so racist they'd refuse to answer questions from a black lawyer. They faced personal humiliation from magistrates who constantly asked them to produce their qualifications at the start of a trial. And having such proof didn't gain them any respect in the outside world. Mandela recalls helping a white woman get out of a tight parking space. She called him 'John' – the name whites gave all black men – and gave him sixpence. When he refused the 'tip' she told him she wouldn't give him a shilling and threw the coin at him.

And then, the ultimate obstacle: the government said they had to move office to a place at a distance from where clients could reach them. They stayed in their office illegally.

Mandela became a bit of a showman in court to overcome the prejudices he and his clients faced. He used flashy gestures, tricksy vocabulary and smart tactics to cross-examine witnesses. Defending a woman accused of stealing her employer's clothes, Mandela went to the exhibits table in the courtroom, picked up a pair of pants on the end of a pencil and asked the employer if these were hers. Embarrassed, she said 'No' and his client's case was dismissed.

It wasn't all courtroom games, of course. The seriousness of the cases that came to Mandela and Tambo meant the two lawyers were fighting for people's lives, homes and livelihoods every day.

One of Johannesburg's biggest shantytowns was Sophiatown. Like Alexandra, it had some old colonial-style buildings. In between were thousands of shacks. More than one family would share a shack and as many as 40 people would share a water tap. Despite this, it was home not only to labourers who had no choice in the matter, but also to writers and doctors, lawyers and artists.

In 1953, the government decided Sophiatown would become a white area and 100,000 black people would be moved elsewhere. Today we talk about the 'gentrification' of an area when it is brought up in the world. South Africa tried to 'gentrify' by force.

Black families found their belongings out on the street and their shacks pulled down. Mandela and

Sisulu were both, for once, free of a banning order and they spoke at an ANC meeting held in a Sophiatown cinema. The police tried to arrest them but Mandela told them to be sure they were still banned before making a wrongful arrest. They hesitated and Mandela and Sisulu were free to speak, alongside Father Trevor Huddleston, a world-famous white anti-*apartheid* campaigner.

The police patrolled inside the cinema with their guns at the ready. They arrested several Indian leaders in the hall and things were getting very tense. The police were just waiting for an excuse to open fire so Mandela began to sing a protest song and the crowd joined in. Disaster was averted.

Many more meetings followed and the police took notes of what was said. Mandela admits he was 'something of a rabble-rousing speaker' and one night he said that the time for passive resistance was over – only violence could end *apartheid*. With the young crowd cheering, he finished with a freedom song and pointed at the police, saying 'There are our enemies'.

This was not a line approved by the ANC executive and Mandela admitted that with no action plan in place, this rabble-rousing wasn't wise. He was in trouble with the leadership and had apologies to make.

There were more apologies needed when he and Walter Sisulu both stepped out of line over the same Sophiatown issue. Sisulu was invited to go to

Bucharest to speak as guest of honour at the World Festival of Youth and Students for Peace and Friendship.

There was no time to ask the ANC executive if he could go – and of course, the government wouldn't have issued him with a passport so there was no point in asking for one. Mandela gave him an official declaration stating his identity and citizenship and Walter headed a small group that travelled to Romania on El Al, the Israeli airline.

Sisulu was in water as deep as Mandela had been over the 'call to arms' speech. Perhaps it was just as well that his unorthodox travel documents got him as far as China and kept him out of the country long enough for the ANC executive to cool down.

The Chinese were supportive of the anti-*apartheid* struggle but thought it was too early to talk of an armed campaign. Looking back, Mandela said they were probably right.

11. The Freedom Charter

MANDELA'S angry speech in the cinema was made just days after a banning order came to an end. When the dust had settled, he drove to the Orange Free State. He was feeling good about being able to drive around the country again – but when he reached his destination, the police were there to greet him. They seemed to take great pleasure in slapping even more restrictive bans on this trouble-maker.

He was banned from going outside of Johannes-burg, was forced to resign from the ANC after ten years at its heart, and could go to no meetings or gatherings for the next two years. This was all enforced under the Suppression of Communism Act, although Mandela was not even a member of the Communist Party.

At 35, he probably saw himself approaching the peak of his political and legal careers. Instead, he was virtually a prisoner in his own home in the Johannesburg area of Orlando, another teeming African township of around 12,000 houses.

Instead of fighting the Sophiatown evictions and leading the ANC against the broader spectrum of *apartheid* oppressions, he was being cut down to size. He had to resign from the ANC at the very moment he'd been up for the national presidency.

Not everyone saw him as the hero, of course. His wife Evelyn, for one, was increasingly disillusioned with this man who seemed to spend more time caring about his country than about his family. At the end of her life she was to say that her 14 years of marriage to Mandela had been 'unhappy'. She blamed his absences and was willing to listen to gossip about relationships with other women. He blamed the fact that she had become a Jehovah's Witness and was increasingly committed to her religion.

Whatever the truth, Mandela being confined to home territory cannot have been a comfortable arrangement.

By now the couple had a fourth child, Maki, and Mandela took the opportunity presented by his banning to bath his three surviving kids and put them to bed. He accepted that if he found himself in prison for defying the restrictions, he would be of no use to his family, his law firm, or the ANC.

If you're thinking that Mandela was not proving to be a very good family man, it is worth looking back at his own childhood. We learn, after all, from example. Until the age of nine, Mandela's own father travelled between the *kraals* of his different wives, spending a short time with each one. His children respected him (although in Mandela's autobiography there is no mention of 'love') but they were used to being raised by their mothers, aunties and grannies.

And then Mandela was taken to live with his guardian, who was very definitely more politician than hands-on dad.

It is easy to see that although Mandela had more modern ideas about marriage and family than his parents' generation, his childhood experiences had prepared him more for life as a public figure than for a nine-to-five job with quality time for the kids.

So it was ironic that at the very time when the bans on his movement meant he had to resign from the ANC leadership, he was in the running to be voted into its top job. He had already written his president-ial address and it was read out by his representative at the conference. In it he said that the old forms of protest were suicidal. It was an impressive speech but it could not put him in the driving seat.

The government then tried to oust Mandela from the legal profession, but the team of lawyers, some of them white Afrikaners, who volunteered to defend him were able to convince the judge to throw out the case.

That meant he could go on fighting publicly for those evicted from Sophiatown, even if his campaign-ing against this on-going ethnic cleansing had to be done underground for the ANC.

It may have been his call for a more extreme approach to the battle for equality that had landed him in more trouble with the authorities, but behind the scenes, Mandela was not slow to insist on pulling in the protesters when the odds were against them.

The authorities played games with the campaigners. In February 1955, the Western Area Resettlement Board pulled forward by three days the first forced removals from Sophiatown. The freedom volunteers wanted to barricade the streets to keep out the enforcers. But Mandela knew that 4,000 armed police and troops had been lined up to 'keep the peace' and so he advised moving families threatened by eviction into safe houses.

This had to be a better option than a massacre, even if as Mandela admitted, the ANC's efforts were too little and too late.

For months, houses were broken up with sledge-hammers after families' meagre belongings had been thrown out on the streets. ANC cells were also broken up and leaders arrested or banned.

There were battles of a different kind over education. There had never been a budget for educating Africans, but the Nationalists twisted the knife even on this issue. The Bantu Education Act was intended, according to the South African Minister of Bantu Education, Dr Henrik Verwoerd, to 'train and teach people in accordance with their opportunities in life'.

All those laws that had been passed to limit black Africans' 'opportunities in life' left them with little need for academic qualifications. And by taking away what little money was available for African schools, this 'Education Act' guaranteed the worst possible schooling for the majority of black children.

School boycotts were planned, but Mandela believed the ANC should take action only if the outcome was achievable. The boycotts would have had to go on indefinitely to have any possible result – and as Verwoerd threatened to close all schools that were boycotted and ban all children who stayed away, the only ones suffering from this protest were the children.

Informal clubs set up to get round the education laws were very successful, with some managing high pass marks. The government of course cracked down – teachers who ran such clubs could be sent to jail. In the end it was seen that a bad education was better than none and the children went to the Bantu schools.

As the 1950s wore on, Mandela often employed this voice of reason as the fight for freedom became more intense. He certainly didn't want to see innocent people put into the firing line – and that is literally what they were facing during any protest.

But eventually, he went back to what he had said in the hot-headed speech that earned him a two-year ban: there was no alternative to armed and violent resistance. As he was to say in his autobiography: 'At a certain point, one can only fight fire with fire.'

Peaceful avenues had been explored. People got very excited by the idea of a Congress of the People that demanded 'Freedom in our lifetime'. Thousands turned up for a meeting in Kliptown, speeches were made, songs sung and ideas exchanged. But on the afternoon of the second day, the police raided the Congress and sent people home. Mandela and Sisulu, both banned, melted into the crowd, which faced the police rifles by singing '*Nkosi Sikel' iAfrika*' – 'God bless Africa'.

The police interviewed every person at the Congress (except those like Mandela and Sisulu who slipped away unseen). The Congress was broken up but the Freedom Charter gave every black South African hope for the future. It condemned government without representation and demanded equal rights and opportunities, and pledged to strive together for democratic change.

The main points of the Freedom Charter were votes for all, equal rights for all, that the people would share in the country's wealth and the land shared by those who worked it. To achieve the demands, the economic and political structure of South Africa would have to be changed and the system of *apartheid* would have to be destroyed.

Meanwhile, *apartheid* was out to destroy the freedom fighters. Raids on offices and homes, bannings, beatings and jail sentences became the norm for all who had a connection with the organisations working to achieve the aims of the Freedom Charter.

12. The Treason Trial & Sharpeville

MANDELA received a five-year ban in 1956, the third that confined him to a small area of Johannesburg and denied him the right to attend meetings and gatherings. Little did he know that he was going nowhere in any case.

In December, he was one of 156 people arrested on charges of high treason and conspiracy to overthrow the government. This was in the wake of the Freedom Charter and all 156 of them faced the death penalty. The accused included the leadership of all the major black, coloured, Indian and anti-*apartheid* organisations. The government didn't miss anyone.

Mandela remembers the loud knocking on his door at dawn on the morning of December 5th. A security officer and two policemen turned his house over for incriminating documents, scaring the children with their heavy-handed tactics. Then they produced the warrant for his arrest. Mandela most regretted that he had been arrested in front of his children, who didn't understand what was going on.

The accused were allowed out of prison if they could pay bail, and to meet those costs, Bishop Ambrose Reeves, novelist Alan Paton (author of *Cry The Beloved Country*), and MP Alex Hepple, the leader of the Labour group in the South African

Parliament, set up a fund. Even bail was set on segregated lines: £250 for whites, £100 for Indians, and £25 for Africans and coloureds.

Some of the country's top lawyers stepped in to defend the accused, including Vernon Berrangé and Bram Fischer. It took a whole year for the preliminary hearings, after which charges against 61 people were dropped. The actual 'Treason Trial' began on August 3rd, 1958.

In between his arrest and the start of the trial, Mandela was divorced and remarried. Evelyn took the opportunity when he was in jail for two weeks to move out.

He had been held with the other prisoners in Johannesburg Prison, known as the Fort. Everyone had to strip naked and line up against a wall. After a white doctor had asked if anyone had any ailments, they were allowed to dress again and taken to two big cells with nothing in them but a floor-level latrine. Each man was given three thin blankets and a sisal mat.

For the two weeks they were held, these cells became what Mandela called 'a convention for far-flung freedom fighters'. These men had all been banned from meetings and gatherings and they had a lot of catching up to do. Some had not even met before because of the bans they had been placed under. It was a most useful, if uncomfortable, time.

The cells rang to freedom songs and intellectual

debate. The men danced traditional Zulu war dances. They bonded and were inspired by their love of country, culture and people.

When they appeared in court, huge crowds came to support them. A special cage had been built in the courtroom to house them, and one of the accused wrote 'Dangerous – Please do not feed' on a piece of paper and stuck it outside the cage. Only an appeal from the lawyers got this barbaric cage removed.

Bail was paid out of the fund and Mandela went home – to an empty house. Evelyn had warned him previously to choose between her and politics. The charge of treason was a step too far for her.

The breakdown of the marriage was obviously painful for the whole family. Thembi, the oldest child, stopped studying. Makgatho slept in Mandela's bed and tried to bring his parents together again. Little Makaziwe just didn't know whether to hug him or run away and Mandela was perhaps most hurt by her confusion.

During the year of the trial hearings, Mandela met a young social worker name Winnie Madikizela and they were married in 1958. The backdrop to this romance was a court piled high with 12,000 submissions of evidence – magazine articles, pamphlets, note-books, letters and scraps of paper that the police had seized from the homes and offices of the accused. Each one of them was presented to the court and numbered.

There were witnesses who were very obviously lying, those who admitted they didn't understand the language that slogans or pamphlets had been written in, and one who was called by the prosecution as an 'expert' in exposing Communism. He identified documents written by a South African Nationalist, two American presidents and himself as Communist propaganda.

Although the defendants faced the death penalty, they became so bored with the proceedings that they resorted to crosswords, games of Scrabble and chess, newspapers, and books. Mandela sometimes brought his own legal work into court and got on with it while the hearing went on around him.

It took just a week into the 'proper' trial, which began in August 1958, for one of the two charges under the Suppression of Communism Act to be dropped. Next, the whole charge was dropped and a new one made against 30 of the accused. Chief Albert Luthuli and Oliver Tambo were released for lack of evidence. Mandela and Sisulu, who at that time was ANC secretary-general, were included in the 30 accused under the new charge.

The trial dragged on and on until on March 29th, 1961. The judge interrupted the defence lawyer as he summed up the evidence. Yes, the ANC wanted to replace the government and had used illegal protests, but there was no evidence that the organisation had used violence and no, the 30 accused were not guilty of treason.

By this time, the firm Mandela and Tambo was falling apart, Mandela was broke and he and Winnie had two children of their own, Zenani and Zindziswa. Winnie was a wife who understood politics and was beginning to be involved in the fight for freedom herself. She perhaps had not realised when she took her vows on June 12th, 1958 that she would soon find herself fighting alone.

In 1960, the ANC was banned as an organisation. When the case against Mandela and his 29 co-accused was finally dismissed, they rejoined a South Africa in which the Nationalists had been re-elected to power and their harsh *apartheid* laws were getting harsher. Now women were included in the pass book laws and could be fined for not carrying them.

Chief Luthuli believed that once women began taking part in the freedom struggle, it could be won. Winnie Mandela was one of those who would lead the women's struggle. With Walter Sisulu's wife Albertina, she took part in a mass female demo against the pass laws and was one of the thousand and more women who were arrested outside the Johannesburg Central Pass Office. She was pregnant but could still give her husband a triumphant smile when he went to visit her in jail. By the next day, another thousand women had been arrested.

Many were not prepared for the hard conditions in jail, but they stuck it out on principle for a fortnight before allowing themselves to be bailed out.

An event that had a much greater impact on the world outside South Africa had also taken place while that lengthy Treason Trial was rumbling on.

Before March 21st, 1960, the name Sharpeville was unknown beyond the Johannesburg township. There had been some disagreement between the ANC and the Pan Africanist Congress (PAC) about how the anti pass book protests should progress, and while the ANC was due to start more mass protests on March 31st, PAC brought their protest forward by ten days. So it was that by 10 o'clock in the morning, between 5,000 and 7,000 men, women and children were outside the local police station, offering themselves up peacefully for arrest because they weren't carrying their pass books.

There are few occasions in an African community when people coming together in a big crowd doesn't lead to singing and dancing, and even at that time in the morning, knowing that many of them would go to jail as a result of their protest, there was a party atmosphere.

There were only 20 police officers inside the station, but the authorities had lined up armoured cars outside and had flown jets overhead to try to disperse the crowd. They wouldn't go. They were there to get arrested and arrested they would be.

At 1.15pm, the police in the armoured cars opened fire on the crowd.

The police said afterwards that some of the crowd

threw stones and inexperienced officers opened fire with their Sten guns and tear gas without orders.

Whatever the truth of the event, the crowd did turn to run away, the police did keep on firing, and most of those who were killed or wounded were shot in the back. No-one ever claimed that anyone in the crowd was armed.

When that day was over, the death toll in Sharpeville was 69. Of those, eight were women and ten were children. Of the 180 and more who were injured, there were 31 women and 19 children.

There were, of course, mass protests, followed by an even tougher government clampdown. More than 18,000 people were detained. It is hard to imagine where the authorities kept all their prisoners.

Outside South Africa, individuals and countries were horrified by the massacre. The United Nations Security Council passed Resolution 134 condemning the police action and South Africa was isolated by country after country. By 1961, it was no longer part of the British Commonwealth. Foreign investors pulled out and 'ordinary' shoppers around the world started to boycott South African goods in earnest.

Inside the country, the PAC and ANC were, of course, banned. The two organisations simply went underground and changed their tactics. There was no appetite any more for the passive protests: that old call to arms made by Mandela during the 1950s was a strategy whose time had come. *Umkhonto we*

Sizwe (Spear of the Nation), the ANC's military organisation that aimed to win the fight for freedom through sabotage, and a military wing of the PAC were soon established.

Despite the fact that they were all on trial, the ANC leaders – including Mandela, Duma Nokwe and Joe Slovo – held an all-night meeting in Johannesburg to decide how to react. They knew that people would want to grieve, and Chief Luthuli agreed with them that there should be a national stay-at-home on March 28th as a day of mourning and protest.

Mandela and Nokwe went out on the streets of Orlando and burned their passes in front of the world media and huge crowds, and Chief Luthuli did the same in Pretoria. Hundreds of thousands of Africans responded to the call for a stay-at-home. In Cape Town, 50,000 gathered in protest. There was rioting and the government declared its State of Emergency.

13. The Brutal Regime

UNDER the new military law, people could be jailed without trial and Mandela was one of 40 thrown into a hell hole of a prison on March 30th. The government wasn't losing any time.

Threatened with violence, treated with disrespect and denied food and bedding for more than 12 hours, it was only when they were told that they were being arrested under Emergency Regulations that they realised a State of Emergency had been called.

Mandela had been hauled out of bed in the early hours of the morning, his house ransacked and then he was bundled into a police vehicle. When he was eventually given sleeping mats and blankets, they were encrusted with dried blood and vomit and covered in lice and cockroaches.

Some 36 hours later, Mandela was on the receiving end of serious verbal abuse from the police. Things looked as though they would turn violent when officers came in to say Mandela and some of the other prisoners had to leave – to attend their on-going treason trial in Pretoria.

Meanwhile, Chief Luthuli himself, who had been arrested in the middle of giving evidence at the trial, had been assaulted by warders. When the judge demanded that he be brought into court, the police refused: whatever rights they believed they had under the State of Emergency, they apparently didn't want their handiwork on an elderly man with a heart complaint to be on public view.

Even in prison, segregation was strict. That meant that the white accused were kept in different prisons from the black accused. The whites got different food from the blacks – there was no sugar for black prisoners, for example, and no bread. Black people weren't supposed to like bread so it was off the menu.

More importantly, the lawyers couldn't get the group together to discuss evidence and tactics. Men and women were not allowed to come together and neither could black and white. Eventually, the accused and their lawyers were allowed to meet, but an iron grille was erected to keep the sexes and colours apart. Helen Joseph, whose name became famous around the world as one of South Africa's white activists, had to be kept apart from Lillian Ngoyi and Bertha Mashaba, two black women accused, and all three had to be kept apart from all of the men.

Peering through the iron grille at each other, Mandela went through court procedure with Helen. In time, he was allowed to visit her in jail at weekends to bring her records of the case, and to speak to other women detainees in his role as a lawyer.

Helen worked within the trades union movement, was a founder member of the Congress of Democrats, which was a strong white ally of the ANC, and of the Federation of South African Women. She was also one of the leaders who read out the clauses of the Freedom Charter at the Congress of the People.

For the female warders in the women's jail, this was a real eye-opener – they didn't know that there were any black lawyers. Mandela hoped that the meetings between the powerful white woman and the black lawyer would chip away at their prejudices.

But his own detainment in prison made the separation from his new family very painful. Winnie was allowed to visit a few times and brought the toddler Zenani with her. The little one couldn't understand why Daddy couldn't leave with them and go home.

When Mandela was called to give testimony, he knew the state wanted to prove that he was a not only a Communist but a leader who preached violence. He made it clear he was not a Communist, but thanked the Communist Party for the support it had given the anti-*apartheid* struggle. He argued with Justice Rumff, the trial judge, who claimed that to be able to vote, a person had to be educated. Mandela said: 'A man looks at a man who will be able to best present his point of view and votes for that man.'

At the end of August, 1960, almost a month after Mandela was called to testify, the State of Emergency was lifted and the accused were allowed to go home for the first time in five months, returning to Pretoria during each week for the court proceedings. The trial went on for another nine months until March 1961.

And back home in Johannesburg, Mandela and other ANC leaders worked in secret to re-establish their now illegal organisation, dissolving the Youth League and Women's League to make it possible for a very limited executive to be able to run the show.

Oliver Tambo had been sent out of the country by the ANC just before the State of Emergency was declared. It was the start of decades of exile for him, but for the ANC and for black South Africa, this had been an excellent move. He was able to drum up support abroad and put plans into action from outside the country's borders.

Perhaps Winnie imagined her husband would be able to spend time with his family. He wasn't. But Winnie was as committed as her husband and happy to name their second daughter Zindziswa after the daughter of Samuel Mqhayi, that inspirational Xhosa poet who had fired up Mandela back in his school days.

In the final days of the trial, in March 1961, Mandela prepared himself to see even less of his family. If he and his fellow accused were found guilty, they would go straight to prison. If they were discharged, it had been decided by the ANC that he would go underground, travelling the country to organise a proposed ANC convention. He later wrote that if a man is not allowed to live the life he believes in, he has no choice but to become an 'outlaw'.

14. The Black Pimpernel

HIS FIVE-YEAR ban was lifted, the court decision would be made the next Monday, and on the night of Saturday, March 25th, Mandela made his first speech for five years in front of 1,400 representatives of 150 different organisations in the town of Pietermaritzburg.

The reaction was mind-blowing: the crowd were right behind him when he called for a national convention involving South Africans of every colour sitting down together to create a constitution that would give them all the equality that the Freedom Charter had set out.

He was elected as honorary secretary to the new National Action Council and he wrote to Prime Minister Verwoerd asking him to call a national constitutional convention. After the cheers and support he'd had at the Pietermaritzburg meeting, the fact that Verwoerd didn't answer the letter and called its contents 'arrogant' in the South African Parliament says a lot more about Verwoerd and the Nationalists than it does about the depth of feeling among the voiceless majority of 1961.

Verwoerd could not have been too happy about the verdict given at the end of the treason trial on

March 27th. The prosecution got a slap on the wrist from the panel of three judges for spending so much time over so much evidence that had led nowhere. It had not proved that the ANC was a Communist organisation, or that the Freedom Charter wanted a Communist state. The accused were found 'not guilty' and discharged.

What a huge chunk this had taken out of everybody's lives. Four years in court, time behind bars, time when movement was restricted, and at the end of it all, joy and relief that could only be experienced momentarily, because now the serious fight began.

With the music of 'Nkosi Silelel' iAfrika' sung by the accused and the triumphant crowds of supporters ringing in his ears, Mandela was about to start a new phase in his life.

Nelson Mandela was now to become known as the Black Pimpernel, reflecting the novel set in the time of The Terror of the French Revolution, when the Scarlet Pimpernel, a hero in disguise, led the authorities a merry dance.

The *Scarlet Pimpernel* had been made into a hit movie in the 1930s and the idea of this leader of the ANC being able to outwit the enemy by using different disguises caught imaginations – particularly in the sympathetic foreign media.

First, Mandela went off round South Africa meeting local and national leaders and staying in safe houses.

He remembered decades later how difficult it was not to be able to be open about anything in his life. He grew a beard and let his hair get longer. He went undercover as a chauffeur, a gardener and a chef. Dressing up as a chauffeur was probably most useful because he could drive from place to place as if he was driving for a non-existent 'master'.

There was a warrant for his arrest and one of his few 'entertainments' was phoning newspaper reporters and feeding them stories about what the 'Black Pimpernel' was doing.

While it was good for the morale of the people for him to pop up at the occasional meeting and make a rousing speech before disappearing again, there were some tricky moments. He was once sitting at traffic lights right next to a police chief he knew well. The disguise of overalls, cap and glasses must have been good, but until the lights turned to green, Mandela's heart was racing.

Much of his work initially was to organise a stay-at-home protest. It was widely publicised and the government was anxious about it. They put Saracen tanks and thousands of police and troops on the streets in advance of the protest. It was the biggest display of military power seen in the country since World War II. There's no doubt that this affected participation in the protest. It takes a brave man to face up to a Saracen tank knowing that another Sharpeville could be the outcome.

Mandela's reaction was to push for the ANC to start a separate military organisation and reluctantly Chief Luthuli agreed. The ANC would still operate a policy of non-violence.

They gave Mandela authority to join up with whoever he wished to create the new organisation, *Umkhonto we Sizwe* (which was to become known as MK), and he brought on board both black and white recruits to help him. Mandela, Joe Slovo and Walter Sisulu were the high command, with Mandela as chairman. They were set to carry out acts of violence that would be damaging to the state but would avoid hurting individuals.

Although he had brought some World War II veterans into MK, he had no idea how to run a guerrilla campaign. Until now he'd been a lawyer with a traditional background that demanded discussion till agreement was reached. Now he was looking at some sort of Che Guevara-style set up with neither funds nor expertise.

Mandela did his research: he read books by military leaders, guerrilla heroes and revolutionaries. He organised practice sessions in a brickworks with explosives. And he hid out in friends' flats and slept on floors. He went jogging in the early dawn then stayed indoors for the rest of the day, almost revealing one hideaway by leaving out milk to go sour (*amasi*, or fermented milk, is a black African favourite) on a white friend's windowsill.

Eventually he went to hide out at Liliesleaf Farm in Rivonia. That's a name to remember.

The buildings had been bought in this rural area on the outskirts of Johannesburg as a safe house for people who, like Mandela, were working undercover. He took the name David Motsamayi and disguised himself as a servant. He made the tea, ran errands and swept the floor. When the real farm workers went home, the MK supporters appeared and plans were discussed for the future.

Security wasn't always tight and allowing Winnie and the children to visit probably wasn't the most professional act – but even a freedom fighter needs to see his family sometimes.

There was no way at this stage that MK could have carried out a revolution. Terrorism wasn't on the agenda: MK and the ANC saw it as a cowardly strategy that could only lose public support at home and around the world. Sabotage – blowing up power plants and telephone lines and railways – was the way to start. No lives were targeted, but this kind of action against essential communications could help bring the economy to its knees. It could work hand in hand with the boycotting of South African goods that supporters outside the country were carrying out with the same intention.

The point of sabotage (and boycott) was to bring the government to the negotiating table.

Sometimes support for a person, a government

or an organisation is difficult to understand. Why, for example, was President Barack Obama given the Nobel Peace Prize in 2009 without having secured peace in any area of the world? Both he and the prize givers were criticised and people said it would have been better to wait until he had achieved something.

Perhaps we should trust the experienced members of the committee that makes the decisions about the peace prize, because with hindsight, we know what an encouragement it was to black South Africans when in 1961, Chief Luthuli was also given the Nobel Peace Prize – when South Africa was far from peace.

In fact, the day after Luthuli came back from Norway, where he had been presented with the prize for working towards peace, MK blew up power stations and government offices in three separate cities around South Africa while flyers were dropped around the country to tell everybody that the Spear of the Nation had been thrown for the first time.

The timing for the Nobel committee was not great, but Mandela had chosen December 16th because it was a day when black Africans mourn the massacre of their people in a battle fought in 1832. The government couldn't decide whether to condemn the sabotage or laugh it off as amateurish, but the white population were certainly scared by the action and the blacks were empowered. At last, they were doing something to make the Nationalists sit up.

It was not quite a peace process, but you have to

get people round a table for discussion somehow.

That same month, the Black Pimpernel was told by the ANC executive to accept an invitation from the Pan-African Freedom Movement for East, Central and Southern Africa (PAFMECSA). It may not have been a catchy name but it was an important organisation and it was meeting in Addis Ababa, the Ethiopian capital.

The conference aimed to bring emerging nations together and support the continent's liberation organisations. Mandela was to seek finance and arms for the South African struggle and with the help of Sisulu, Kathrada and Duma Nokwe, he was given papers and taken to Bechuanaland (which became Botswana in 1966) to charter a plane for Dar es Salaam in Tanzania (or Tanganyika as the country was called then).

That first leg of the journey to Ethiopia did not go smoothly. Both Sisulu and Nokwe were arrested on their way to take Mandela to his plane, and Mandela had to stay two weeks in Bechuanaland before he could be welcomed in Dar es Salaam.

There were many potential dangers and plans had to be changed and changed again. A water-logged airstrip, rogue elephants and a lioness heading towards their open parked vehicle were perhaps welcome diversions to rumours of kidnappings and arrests by security forces.

Once up in the air, Mandela was out of the clutches

of the South African police, but it was no easy ride. The Victoria Falls, discovered by the Scottish explorer and missionary David Livingstone and named after his queen, are a spectacular wall of water stretching along the borders between modern-day Zambia and Zimbabwe. When Mandela made this flight, they were still the British colonies of Northern and Southern Rhodesia. The route then went north and east through mountains to reach an airstrip just over the Northern Rhodesian border in Tanganyika. For today's traveller flying in a small modern aircraft, the journey can still be hair-raising. For Mandela, who had never stepped inside an aircraft before, the turbulence was alarming.

More alarming still was the fact that the pilot couldn't raise anyone at his destination. There was thick mist in the mountains and he brought the plane down low to follow a road rather than trust to his navigational instruments. When the road itself disappeared and the pilot made a quick U-turn, Mandela took courage to look out and saw that a mountain had reared up in front of the plane.

His fear was justified. The alarms went off and Mandela and a tight-lipped Joe Slovo prepared to meet their Maker.

Instead, the plane bobbed out into clear skies and the pilot made a safe landing in a country that intrigued Mandela because on December 6th, 1961, just two months before his visit, Tanganyika had received its independence from the British.

He found a very different atmosphere to the one at home. Here, a black skin was not something that relegated its owner to the bottom level of society. The country was ruled by Africans and here he was free to do as he pleased. He was allowed to walk through the front door of the hotel and was called 'sir' by the white hotel receptionist.

Not everything went the way he would have wished. His meeting with President Julius Nyerere didn't bring the support for armed struggle that he had hoped for and he found that the ANC's rival organisation, the Pan Africanist Congress (PAC) held more appeal for the newly elected president.

The next leg of Mandela's journey took him to Sudan, where his very basic 'travel document' stating his name and the fact that he had permission to return to Tanganyika, was accepted with a smile and a welcome by the immigration officer. He had to use all his diplomatic skills to get his white companions into the country without passports – no black man could understand why a white man would travel without official documents.

From Sudan, the little South African entourage went to Nigeria for a conference in Lagos that was intended to unite African states but was little more than a talking shop. There he met up with Oliver Tambo, who during his exile has set up ANC offices in England, Egypt, Ghana and Tanganyika and had created good relationships in each country. Now they were to head on to Ethiopia, stopping off to change planes in Khartoum as they passed through Sudan again.

The surprise he had there was that the pilot was black. He realised just how low his horizons had become because of the *apartheid* mentality. Why shouldn't a black African be a pilot – or a president, like Julius Nyerere?

Mandela got a good reception from many of the African leaders at the PAFMECSA conference. Here he also found black generals running the army, black leaders taking their seats at the conference, and a black Emperor – Haile Selassie.

This was the Black Pimpernel's first public appearance since he had left South Africa. He explained that in his own country he had lived like an outlaw for the previous ten months. But he swore he would go back to join the fight against *apartheid*, and won even more hearts and minds with that declaration.

It was clear now to all the other African leaders that MK would step up the sabotage. Some approved, some were reluctant to back Mandela.

When the conference finished, Mandela did not go back to South Africa immediately. He set off on a whistlestop tour of sympathetic African states.

In Egypt he saw a state with an army, navy and air force – and a history of culture and splendour that knocked on the head any idea that Africans had no civilised past. In Tunisia, he was offered money for weapons and training for MK soldiers. In Morocco, leaders explained how they organised their resistance to their French colonial masters. In Algeria, he was advised not to neglect politics in favour of guerrilla warfare.

He flew in ramshackle planes to Mali and Guinea, with chickens pecking in the aisle and women selling their produce. In Liberia, there was more money for weapons and training – and then for ten days he spent time in England, talking with sympathetic MPs and South Africans in exile.

Mandela then went back to Ethiopia to do six months' military training. This was cut short to eight weeks because the action was hotting up in South Africa and the ANC wanted its military leader back.

Back in Dar es Salaam, he met up with 21 MK recruits. He insisted that these men receive political training as well as military training because his aim was to create an equal society, not a bunch of thugs who could assassinate a president. He wanted them to understand that they were the future of a fair and free South Africa.

If the journey into Tanganyika had been scary, the journey back to South Africa was doubly so, but for different reasons. The South African authorities had been made aware that Mandela was on his way. After admitting his true identity to a magistrate who turned out to be sympathetic, he drove from Botswana into South Africa posing as the chauffeur of Cecil

Williams, a white theatre director who was a member of MK.

With directions from Williams, Mandela managed to reach Liliesleaf Farm at Rivonia the next morning. He held a secret meeting with some of the top ANC and MK men and they brought each other up to date.

He wanted the ANC to lead the Congress Alliance and headed to Durban to meet Chief Luthuli, still the leader of the ANC. There were other discussions and reunions with supporters. Heading back to Johannesburg on August 5th, 1962, and still wearing his white chauffeur's coat although he and Williams were sharing the driving, Mandela looked round to see two carloads of white men following them. Somebody had tipped off the police.

They decided to stop, rather than risk being fired at. Mandela hid his revolver and notebook full of MK details in the upholstery of the car and got out. He gave his 'David Motsamayi' identity, but the police sergeant was having none of it. Mandela and Williams were arrested and taken to Pietermaritzburg where they were locked in separate cells.

Next day he was taken to Johannesburg. Near the city, nice cops turned into nasty cops. On the journey, they had let Mandela have a brief walk and some food. Now they clapped him in handcuffs, shoved him into a police van and drove him to jail in a showy motorcade.

He found himself in a cell close to Walter Sisulu

and next day he was taken to court and charged. He'd been on the run for 17 months and was top of the 'wanted' list. The charges this time were illegal exit from the country and incitement to strike.

To make sure that the Black Pimpernel could not escape, he was kept in the prison hospital, which the authorities considered to be safe from any break-out. There were stories that he had been betrayed by a white man or an Indian – claims that Mandela believed to be plants by the government to stir up trouble between the different anti-*apartheid* organisations.

In 1990, a retired Central Intelligence Agency officer told a news agency that the CIA used a plant inside the ranks of the ANC to tip off the South African authorities about Mandela's whereabouts. The American secret service wanted to close down the ANC's activities because they believed Africa was being destabilised by such organisations.

Whatever the truth, Mandela was transferred to a jail in Pretoria and then back to Johannesburg. He used his time to study for the law degree that would allow him to practise as an advocate.

When he eventually was taken to court on October 15th, 1962, there were mass 'Free Mandela' demonstrations. The authorities had made it known his case would be heard in Johannesburg, then switched to the Pretoria court at the last moment. Joe Slovo, who was to act as his legal adviser, was banned and couldn't leave Johannesburg, so Bob Hepple (now

Professor Sir Bob Hepple), another white man who was involving himself in the freedom struggle, took Slovo's place.

Mandela decided to make this a show trial that would air the grievances of the ANC.

He went into court wearing the traditional Xhosa leopard-skin *kaross*, and Winnie wore a traditional headdress and skirt. The Mandelas' appearance and the spontaneous clenched-fist salute from everyone packed into the courtroom were a potent mix. '*Amandla!*' the crowd shouted. '*Ngawethu!*' was the response – 'Power!' 'The power is ours!'

Back in the cells, Mandela learned the full power of his traditional dress. The commanding officer of the jail demanded that he hand it over. Mandela refused. The commanding officer called the magnificent leopard skin a 'blanket'. Instead of being diminished by the insult, Mandela was all the more determined not to part with the *kaross*. Eventually, he was allowed to wear it in court, but not going to or coming from the building in case it stirred up the crowds.

He was allowed to address the court and made a passionate speech in which he said that the case was a 'trial of the aspirations of the African people'. He questioned whether an all-white court could offer him balanced justice and he condemned racial discrimination.

Over a hundred witnesses testified that he had left the country illegally and that he had incited African workers to go on strike in May 1961. He did not dispute either charge.

His unanswered letter to Prime Minister Verwoerd was produced in evidence and the Prime Minister's private secretary, Mr Barnard, was called as a witness. Mandela, conducting his own defence, asked in cross-examination if this letter was not of vital concern to the majority of South African citizens, dealing as it did with issues of human rights and civil liberties. Mr Barnard said he did not think it was important.

Mandela took Barnard through all of the issues step by step. Was there a black Member of Parliament? Could black people vote? Could they be members of provincial and municipal councils? The answers to all of these questions was, of course, 'No'.

Barnard was then asked if he would agree that in any civilised country, it would be 'scandalous' for the prime minister to ignore a letter about such issues affecting the majority of the citizens of that country. He could not bring himself to agree, however often Mandela returned to the question, and would only say that the prime minister did not answer it because it was aggressive and discourteous.

Mandela called no witnesses, and told the court he was guilty of no crime. Overnight, he heard that the General Assembly of the United Nations had voted in favour of sanctions against South Africa and that MK had carried out acts of sabotage. The outside world was with Mandela. MK was with Mandela. Even the prosecutor in this case was with him, and told him so in a private conversation.

He walked into court with his clenched fist held high, calling out *'Amandla!'* The crowd in the court responded *'Ngawethu!'* and the sound shook the building.

He made a speech (a 'plea of mitigation') that lasted an hour and reminded the court that this land had once belonged to the African. He explained why he had joined the ANC and why all men of conscience had to fight against oppression and strive for the good of society. He said the government had driven him outside of society and that in the future, people would say that he was innocent and that members of the government should have been brought before the court instead of him.

Sentenced to five years in jail (three for inciting people to strike and two for leaving the country without a passport), Mandela again raised his fist in salute and called *'Amandla!'* three times. Then spontaneously, the crowd in the court sang *'Nkosi Sikelel' iAfrika'*. People danced and women ululated. It felt like a triumph – and in a way it was, because Mandela had spoken and the world was able to listen.

Now he was silenced.

15. First Sight of Robben Island

MANDELA had told the court: 'I detest racialism because I regard it as a barbaric thing, whether it comes from a black man or a white man.'

The barbarism that he was to experience after leaving that courtroom was grounded in a racism that saw the black man as intellectually and socially challenged – as a creature to be reviled, patronised, used and abused.

They made him strip, took his magnificent *kaross* and gave him prison gear, which included – as for all Africans – a pair of short trousers. These were not the holiday shorts we are comfortable with today. They were the kind of shorts a little boy would wear to school and they were designed to put the African prisoner in his place.

Mandela objected, of course. He complained about the food, too. And Colonel Jackson, head of the Pretoria prison, offered him a deal. If he wanted to wear his own clothes and eat his own food, he would have to be kept in solitary confinement.

He agreed, and found himself locked up 23 hours a day, with two half-hour periods of exercise. He saw no-one except the warder and he had no window in his cell. A light burned day and night and he had no way of telling the time. He had nothing to read and no means of writing. Eventually, the solitude got to him and he gave back his long trousers so that he could talk to somebody. He found himself alongside the other political prisoners held in the jail.

Walter Sisulu, who had also been on trial in Johannesburg for incitement to strike, was brought to the Pretoria prison at the start of his six-year sentence, but his lawyers were appealing against the sentence and he was released on bail.

Outside, life went on. The government turned the screw on the freedom fighters and the freedom fighters held their meetings in secret.

Inside, Mandela was beginning to get used to the rhythm of Pretoria jail. Then without warning and with just ten minutes to pack his things, Mandela was on the move. He was taken with three other political prisoners to Cape Town, a journey that took over 12 hours. The prisoners were handcuffed together and pushed into the back of a van with one bucket as a toilet. It was a long, embarrassing and disgusting journey to Cape Town docks. Still chained, they were put below decks on an old wooden ferry bound for the most notorious prison in South Africa – Robben Island. On the way across the seven kilometres of choppy sea, the warders took great delight in peeing on them from the deck above.

Robben Island looked very beautiful from a distance. As long ago as 1658, it had been a place where Europeans kept their African prisoners and only one was said to have escaped. Later it became a place where people with the disease leprosy were sent. Then people with mental health problems were isolated there. From 1939 to 1959 it was a naval base, but in 1961, just the year before Mandela and his fellow political prisoners were sent there, it had been turned into a maximum security prison.

There was barbed wire on top of its massive walls, a watch tower with armed guards, and in the maximum security building the long corridors were lined with cells that had bars on the windows and barred doors that allowed no privacy.

The island was scarred by a lime quarry where regular prisoners worked each day as part of their 'hard labour' sentences.

It was the way that prisoners were treated, rather than their physical conditions, which led to Mandela calling it 'without question the harshest, most iron-fisted outpost of the South African penal system'. It was the regime at the prison (designed by the Nationalist government) that gave it the label, 'hell-hole of *apartheid*'.

From the moment Mandela and his companions landed on Robben Island, the warders made it clear what they would be subjected to. Racist jibes, orders issued in language usually used for farm animals, and deliberately abusive treatment were all handed out in the few minutes it took to get from the jetty to the reception building. The floor of the reception room was inches deep in water and the prisoners were told to strip. As each garment came off, the guards gave it the once-over then threw it in the water. Then they told the prisoners to get dressed again.

And of course, they called these men 'Boy!' The lawyer Mandela was no exception. One of the officers in charge of the warders turned on him for questioning regulations and not only screamed the insult at him but physically threatened him.

Mandela admitted later that this was a frightening experience, but even so he stood up to this threatening bully and in turn threatened him – with the 'highest court in the land'. He told this officer that while he was ready to serve his five years, he would not be bullied.

It turned out that Colonel Steyn, commanding officer of Robben Island, was not informed that his new batch of inmates were political prisoners, who under international law must be treated with respect. Knowing how cruel the warders were to the political prisoners, it's hard to imagine what the criminal inmates suffered.

The four political prisoners were put into a single cell with toilets and showers, but there were only mats to sleep on and cold porridge for supper. A sympathetic coloured warder brought them news of the outside world (Mandela's wife had not been told of his transfer, according to the newspapers) but there were vicious Afrikaans warders who took pleasure in assaulting prisoners and humiliating them.

As quickly as Mandela had been transferred from the mainland to Robben Island, his fellow prisoners were told to pack up and disappeared, leaving Mandela alone, uneasy and vulnerable. Then he was moved back to Pretoria. No reason was given why, but in July, 1963, he found that he was in good company in Pretoria local jail.

Called to the prison office, he was surprised to see Walter Sisulu, Govan Mbeki, Ahmed Kathrada, Andrew Mlangeni, Bob Hepple, Raymond Mhlaba, Elias Motsoaledi, Dennis Goldberg, Rusty Bernstein and Jimmy Kantor. These were all men who were either in the high command of the ANC or MK, or were members of other anti-apartheid movements.

Each of them was charged with sabotage. This was nine months into Mandela's five-year sentence.

16. Another Trial

FOR MONTHS the authorities had been tapping phones, carrying out a round-the-clock watch on suspects, and finally carried out a raid on Liliesleaf Farm in Rivonia to arrest the remainder of the accused. They had lifted all sorts of papers at the farm and felt they could congratulate themselves on rounding up the country's leading freedom fighters – or terrorists as they would have classed them.

A team of top anti-*apartheid* lawyers volunteered their services, but until they had already been charged in court, Mandela was not allowed to speak to them because he was a convicted prisoner. Finally he was able to take part in a consultation with Bram Fischer, Vernon Berrangé, Joel Joffe, George Bizos and Arthur Chaskalson.

The government had already told the lawyers that they were seeking the death penalty and the accused had no reason to think they would get away with less. The warders took sadistic delight in telling Mandela he was going for the 'long sleep'.

The case began at the Supreme Court in Pretoria on October 9th, 1963. Despite each prisoner being led into court by two armed guards, each man gave the ANC salute as he emerged from the cells. The crowd in the visitors' gallery shouted the freedom cries – and had their names and photographs taken by the police as a result.

Joel Joffe, who after working as a civil rights lawyer in South Africa went on to become chair of the charity Oxfam, and later a Labour member of the UK House of Lords, recalled that as Mandela came up the stairs to the dock, there was a 'ripple of excitement' from the public benches. His deep voice boomed out the African National Congress battle cry 'Amandla'. A large part of the audience, the African audience, replied immediately in chorus 'Ngawthu'.

The police obviously hadn't expected this reaction and were rattled. They'd tried to fill the benches with off-duty warders and police officers and didn't think so many supporters could have got in to cause this dramatic start to the case. As the room also had its fair share of foreign media correspondents and members of foreign governments, this was an embarrassment.

Mandela looked thin and ill and was humiliated by having to appear in his prison uniform of shorts and sandals. Although he had not known it, his fellow accused had been in solitary confinement for three months and were equally frail. But the response to Mandela's freedom cry from the gallery was enough to send their spirits soaring. The same answer came as each prisoner emerged from the depths of the Supreme Court building into the dock, gave the same clenched fist salute and cried out 'Amandla'.

The Judge-President of the Transvaal, Dr Quartus de Wet, presided over the case and the prosecutor was Dr Percy Yutar.

Dr Yutar called witness after witness to back up the claims of the charges that the accused had organised acts of sabotage and incited others to carry out acts of sabotage with the aim of bringing down the government. They were accused of planning armed and violent revolution and receiving money from inside and outside the country to carry out their campaign. There were also charges under the Suppression of Communism Act.

Mandela was accused of committing 156 acts of sabotage – while he was in jail.

The defence team were able to show that some of these witnesses had been tortured to get them to make statements against the accused. One witness said he was beaten, a bag put over his head and that he was subjected to electric shocks until he signed a statement. Other witnesses were proven to be liars. Others still were undercover policemen who gave the 'right' answers to the prosecution.

The same sort of obstacles were put in the way of the defence team and the defendants as had been experienced during the Treason Trial that had led to Mandela's five-year jail sentence. Added to this, Dr Yutar often, according to Joel Joffe, presented the case for the prosecution in a bizarre and unprofess-ional way.

Despite the restrictions placed on meetings and consultations, the lawyers got to know the accused well and Joffe says in his book about the trial (*The State vs. Nelson Mandela: the trial that changed South Africa*) that Mandela had all the qualities of a leader. His engaging personality, calm bearing, tact, diplomacy and conviction made his fellow accused not surprisingly turn to him to be their spokesperson.

Joffe wrote: 'When I first met him, I found him attractive and interesting. By the time the case finished I regarded him as a really great man.'

Ironically, after all the trouble the government had taken to produce evidence to convict – all the torture, the 'grooming' and intimidation of witnesses and their families, the straightforward dishonesty of regular criminals recruited to damn the accused – the accused themselves decided that rather than fight the charges, they would use the trial to make their case against the government.

Kathrada spoke about the harassment people suffered. Govan Mbeki recalled the police raids and violence against innocent citizens that had blighted his childhood. Some recounted the details of the Sophiatown evictions, exposing to the world's media the South African government's policy of ethnic cleansing.

Each stood up to cross examination remarkably well, never losing their tempers, never incriminating their fellow accused or others, and never denying their involvement with the ANC or MK. Each accused explained at length why they had come to be a member of such organisations, and in the eyes of the foreign media this helped to create a picture of the horrific impact of *apartheid*.

Around the world, support was growing for the accused and for the whole campaign to bring this oppressive system to an end.

The defence set out to prove that MK was a separate organisation from the ANC, that the ANC was not a 'tool' of the Communist Party, and that MK had not adopted a plan to prepare for guerrilla warfare, and that although guerrilla warfare was considered, the hope of the leaders of MK was to avoid such action.

Dr Yutar believed he could make the case for the Nationalists by goading the accused. He was obviously gearing up to cross examine Mandela and trip him up in lies and deceit – but Mandela, after great discussion with the legal team and his fellow accused, chose not to go into the witness box but instead to make a statement from the dock.

This meant that he could not be cross examined.

Mandela had spent weeks preparing his statement and he read it quietly and slowly. As he went on, the court grew more and more quiet, until, as Joel Joffe described it, 'it seemed that no-one in the court dared move or breathe'.

Like his fellow accused, he explained his own background and why that led to his membership of the ANC and MK. He denied nothing about his own role in MK. He described the way Africans lived in South Africa, and finished with a summary of what the ANC wanted for Africans.

This part of his statement has become as well-known as the 'I have a dream. . .' speech which had been made by American civil rights campaigner Dr Martin Luther King some eight months previously, on August 26th, 1963 in Washington DC.

Using the same repetitive rhetoric that King became famous for, Mandela told the court – and the world:

> 'Africans want to be paid a living wage. Africans want to perform work which they are capable of doing, not work which the government declares them to be capable of. Africans want to be allowed to live where they obtain work, and not be endorsed out of an area because they were not born there. Africans want to be able to own land in places where they work, and not be obliged to live in rented houses which they can never call their own. Africans want to be part of the general population, and not confined to living in their own ghettos. African men want to have their wives and children to live with them where they work, and not be forced into an unnatural existence in men's hostels. African women want to be with their menfolk and not left permanently

widowed in the reserves. Africans want to be allowed out after 11 o'clock at night and not to be confined to their rooms like little children. Africans want to be allowed to travel in their own country and to seek work where they want to and not where the Labour Bureau tells them. Africans want a just share in the whole of South Africa; they want security and a stake in society.'

He went on to say that Africans wanted equal political rights, which he said he knew was a revolutionary idea to white people and that white people feared democracy because the majority of voters would be Africans.

He told the court that this was the only way to achieve racial harmony and freedom for all; that the ANC had spent half a century fighting against racialism.

He said: 'During my lifetime I have dedicated myself to the struggle of the African people. I have fought against white domination and I have fought against black domination. I have cherished the ideal of a democratic and free society in which all persons live together in harmony and with equal opportunities.'

And knowing that Mr Justice de Wet could well sentence him to death at the end of this trial, he finished by saying: 'It is an ideal which I hope to live for and to achieve. But if needs be it is an ideal for which I am prepared to die.'

17. Second Journey to Robben Island

DURING THE TRIAL, the United Nations had taken an almost unanimous vote calling for the immediate release of the Rivonia accused. Almost? South Africa voted against the resolution. The ten accused had generally admitted plotting to overthrow the South African government, but they had received a medal for meritorious service to the cause of peace from the World Peace Council.

And Mandela was elected president of the Students' Union of London University.

Within South Africa, the writer Alan Paton, author of the anti-*apartheid* novel *Cry the beloved country*, agreed to speak on their behalf in court before the judge passed sentence, despite the fact that he was a pacifist and these were men who were admitting to considering violence against the state.

The support for the accused spread around the world like a wave. The South African government was not happy.

Mr Justice de Wet, however, had little patience with Dr Yutar's summing up, demanding: 'You do concede that you failed to prove guerrilla warfare was ever decided upon, do you not?' As a result of this rebuff, Yutar became almost hysterical and tried to blame even the Sharpeville massacre on the ANC.

The more professional approach of the defence lawyers brought some dignity back into the court room. Nothing, of course, was going to change the verdict. What were at stake now were these men's lives. The judge adjourned the case for three weeks to consider the verdict.

When he returned, he found Mandela, Sisulu, Goldeberg, Mhlaba, Mlangeni, Motsoaledi and Mbeki guilty on all charges. Kathrada was found guilty of one of the charges, and Bernstein was found not guilty.

As they were taken out of the court, Walter Sisulu's wife Albertina led the crowd in singing *Nkosi Silelel' iAfrika*. As the vans appeared outside the court carrying the prisoners back to jail to wait for sentencing next morning, a roar went up from the crowd: '*Amandla!*' The prisoners' clenched fists came through the bars of the vans and they shouted back '*Ngawethu!*'

All the prisoners had decided that they would not appeal against the death sentence. Sisulu, Mbeki and Mandela believed that to appeal against any sentence would undermine the moral stance they had taken – that they had acted as they had for moral reasons.

But just as they had all used the trial to get their

beliefs across to the world, they wanted to use the day of sentencing to remind the world that, in Mandela's words, 'no sacrifice was too great in the struggle for freedom'.

The lawyers told them they could speak if Mr Justice de Wet passed the death sentence and Mandela said he would have a lot to say. He wanted to die – if die he had to – knowing that his death would be an 'inspiration to the cause for which I was giving my life'.

They all expected to be given the death sentence. They felt that was the only way to be properly prepared for it. 'We were all prepared, not because we were brave but because we were realistic,' Mandela said.

So on Friday June 12th, 1964, almost a year after the raid on Rivonia, the accused went to court to hear their fate. Mandela's wife and mother were in court, as were many families of the accused. The tension for them could have been no less than for the prisoners. Mandela understood that his mother must have been experiencing indescribable emotions as she waited to know if her son was to hang.

Mr Justice de Wet was insulting in his speech that day. He said he was not convinced that these men acted purely for the good of the people – would they not be the ones in power if their campaign was successful?

But his sentence was not death. 'The sentence,' de

Wet said in such a quiet voice that the accused could not catch it, 'in the case of all the accused will be one of life imprisonment.'

There was to be no speech – that was reserved for those condemned to death.

Instead, the accused were bundled out of court with scarcely the chance for an ANC salute. The police were jumpy, and quite rightly so. They had to get these men away from the Supreme Court through thousands of ANC and MK supporters, and a few hundred apartheid protesters – many of them white South African students who were running against the tide of opinion held by most young people around the world.

There were the usual cries of support, so perfectly delivered that they sounded rehearsed and so powerful that people felt the vibration in their souls. After half an hour, the police decided to make a break for it and drove the prisoners' van out through the crowds, the prisoners raising clenched fists through the vehicle's bars.

Dennis Goldberg, as a white man, was taken to another prison, while the rest were locked up in Pretoria Local. After the celebratory mayhem – because the crowds were very definitely celebrating that their heroes would live and not hang – the echoing silence of the prison, broken only by the clang of steel doors, sobered the Rivonia trial prisoners.

Mandela had time to reflect as he tried to sleep on

the cement floor on his sisal mat. It was clear that de Wet had made his decision because of all the pressure being put on the South African government from around the world.

There were protests by politicians in the UK, the US and the USSR (as Russia was in 1964). Dockers on quaysides in many countries were threatening to strike rather than handle South African goods – shoppers weren't even going to be given the opportunity to make their own choices because the fruit, cigarettes and other goods just weren't going to get through.

In Britain, the boycott of goods had been going on for some years – Labour Party leader Hugh Gaitskell had gone on TV in 1960 to urge more people to back the boycott. The Labour Party had also been calling for South Africa to be thrown out of the Common-wealth since 1955. At the 1958 Cardiff Common-wealth Games, South Wales miners protested at the presence of the all-white South Africans, and that had set a precedent – cricket and rugby teams, boxers and athletes began to refuse to compete against South Africa, whether on their home territory or in South Africa itself.

The presentation of international awards in favour of the anti-*apartheid* movement that had so pointedly been announced during the year of the Rivonia Trial was isolating the country still further.

To sentence these men to death would have been

political, social and economic suicide for South Africa. Prime Minister Verwoerd may have boasted that he was throwing all the telegrams of protest in the bin, but de Wet saw the sense of a life sentence.

It seemed that the whole of Pretoria prison sang that night. Freedom songs rang out until lights out, when the cries of '*Amandla!*' went up and hundreds of voices replied '*Ngawethu!*'

Then Mandela and the rest got the midnight call to move. Seven of them were handcuffed and bundled into the back of a van for a journey Mandela remembered only too well from his previous imprisonment. As the van set off, they sang and discussed the trial. They were given drinks and sandwiches and a friendly warden suggested that they wouldn't be in jail long because of the swell of international protest. He saw them getting a heroes' welcome to freedom in a couple of years.

He was wrong.

In fact, the journey was not as Mandela remembered, because this time the van took them a much shorter distance to a military airport, where they were transferred to a tiny plane that took them down to Cape Town and then over to Robben Island itself. The rest were afraid of flying. Mandela, still nervous but at least experienced, used the time to make a note of places where MK could engage in a guerrilla campaign.

It was freezing cold, but all of them except

Kathrada (who was, of course, from an Indian background) were issued with shorts. They all were given shoes – an improvement on the sandals Mandela had previously been given – but only Kathrada was given socks.

For the first few days they stayed in the old jail, before being transferred to the new maximum security fortress with its 20-foot high wall and three lines of cells around a quadrangle. The Rivonia Seven were sent to B wing and given individual cells that were dripping with damp. The cells had a window, an entrance with a metal grill and a heavy wooden door, and each man was given a felt mat and a sisal one to sleep on. Mandela remembers that it was so cold they slept full dressed.

The cell was just six feet across, so a tall man could touch each two-foot thick wall with both head and feet when he lay down.

Outside in the corridor, a card labelled the prisoner in each cell: Nelson Mandela – 466/64. The number signified that he was the 466th prisoner to be admitted to the island in 1964.

18. The Fruits of Freedom

SECTION B became the political wing of the prison. In another building, around 1,000 general prisoners were held. The government didn't want the political prisoners giving the criminals ideas.

In the first few months, the 20 or so political prisoners began working on stone breaking. They had to sit in the courtyard, each man with his pile of boulders. The boulders were delivered by lorry and the prisoners wheeled barrow loads to the centre of the courtyard. Then with either a four-pound hammer or a fourteen-pound hammer, depending on the size of the stones, they had to crush the boulders into gravel.

The biggest nod towards safety was make-shift wire masks that were supposed to protect their eyes from flying chips of stone.

Silence was strictly enforced by patrolling warders. At lunchtime, they were given a stinking soup to warm them; the temperature hovered around 4°C. By week two, the Rivonia Seven had instigated a go-slow.

Mandela found a much harsher regime in place than during his brief imprisonment there in 1962. The warders were now all Afrikaaners, tough, cruel and racist. He tried to develop strategies that would help them all to avoid having their spirit broken – a main aim of the regime. He was glad that the prison authorities kept them all together, because they were able to support each other.

It was the little details that challenged most. The iron buckets that were their toilets had concave lids that were supposed to hold the water for washing. The porridge for breakfast was delivered by general prisoners, who spun a bowl into each cell that the Rivonia Seven tried hard to catch without losing any of the porridge. Having their jackets fastened properly for inspection each morning, lifting their caps in an enforced respectful gesture to the warders, being sent to solitary confinement because the warder decided a cell was untidy – these were the degrading daily issues they had to put into perspective to remain sane.

Mandela was known as a troublemaker – that name Rolihlahla really was prophetic – by the warders. When the group was transferred to work in another place on the island quarrying lime, he led protests for better conditions.

He even acted as lawyer for the general prisoners, some of whom were brutally beaten by guards. Sometimes he achieved results, sometimes the brutality continued. Mandela also supported young members of PAC who found themselves imprisoned on Robben Island and managed to politicise some of the general prisoners.

The Rivonia Seven were allowed to study, and Mandela enrolled with the University of London. The authorities would not allow him to have some of the recommended books. However, this permission to study came with a desk (in reality a wide shelf) and chair.

Getting news of the outside world was tricky. There were occasional visits from the International Red Cross, but the authorities made sure that even the food improved in the days before representatives arrived. Visits from wives and families could be years apart (Mandela saw Winnie three months after his arrival on the island and then not for another two years). When they went to work in the quarry, they tried to retrieve the newspaper that the warders' sandwiches were wrapped in, and very occasionally, they were able to bribe a warder to give them a newspaper.

That led to trouble for them and the bribed warders, so it wasn't a regular practice. Being isolated for weeks because you've read a ham-smeared news story is no joke.

The news these men were missing was that rather than the government softening up to soothe inter-national opinion, *apartheid* laws were becoming tougher and tougher. The Terrorism Act of 1967 was far more frightening than the 90-day detention process that had allowed police to hold someone without being charged for three months. Now someone could be held in custody indefinitely and no-one had the right even to inquire about them. People could be 'disappeared'.

As time went on, the Robben Island political prisoners became more organised and were able to receive more information. Sometimes this was smuggled to them; sometimes they were allowed newspapers and magazines.

They did, of course, hear the news about the death of 12-year-old Hector Pietersen and all those young people shot by the police in Soweto when they tried to protest about being forced to do school lessons in Africaans. That was twelve years into their sentence.

And they did hear about Solomon Kalushi Mahlangu. Solomon was, like Hector, one of the students who joined the peaceful protest against the imposition of Afrikaans. As well as the death toll that day in Soweto, the 575 who had died by the end of 1976 and the thousands who had been wounded in the conflict, 21,000 people were prosecuted for their part in the protests that followed the massacre.

According to ANC records, thousands then left the country to escape the detentions and bannings, believing they could continue the struggle better from outside South Africa.

Among them was Solomon Mahlangu, then 19, who ran off in the night without telling his mother where he was going. He trained as a soldier and returned the next year to join MK. On his way to a student protest commemorating the Soweto massacre the year before, he was swooped on by the police, along with his co-MK workers Monty Motloung and George 'Lucky' Mahlangu. The Johannesburg police opened fire and two white civilians were killed. By this time, the police were trigger happy and violence on the streets had become an everyday occurrence.

George managed to get away. Monty was so badly beaten up by the police that he was left with severe brain damage and wasn't even able to appear at his own trial. Solomon hadn't fired a shot but ended up facing murder charges on his own. His lawyers weren't told that his trial had started. No surprise, then, that he was found guilty.

On March 2, 1977, his response to the death sentence was '*Amandla!*' The new generation had truly picked up Mandela's baton and was fighting for the cause that had jailed the Rivonia Trial accused for life. For the next two years, the international community campaigned to have Solomon's death sentence overturned. There was a call for the recognition of all South African freedom fighters as prisoners of war.

South Africa stood firm. On April 6th, 1979, at the age of 23, Solomon Mahlangu was hanged. As he stood on the gallows he gave the ANC salute, and the ANC reports his final words as: 'My blood will nourish the tree that will bear the fruits of freedom. Tell my people that I love them. They must continue the fight.'

The ANC dedicated a school to Solomon and the young people of South Africa joined the democratic world in taking up the fight for freedom with even more determination. The International Defence and Aid Fund and the Anti Apartheid Movement campaigned tirelessly for those detained without a trial and for decent conditions for convicted prisoners.

This relentless pressure on the regime in South Africa eventually brought its rewards. Mandela was moved in April 1984 to Pollsmoor Prison in Cape Town and then to the Victor Verster Prison near the town of Paarl, some 60 kilometres inland from Cape Town on what today is the north eastern fringe of a national park.

Throughout these moves, Mandela was carrying out talks with the South African government, sometimes secretly, sometimes with the full knowledge of his fellow prisoners and the ANC executive.

The talks were never easy and he turned down offers of remission on his sentence in exchange for acceptance of some of the government's policies. He also refused to renounce violence, saying that prisoners could not enter into contracts – only free men could negotiate.

Professor Tom Lodge, who has written an account of Mandela's life, questioned how this man could remain influential throughout the 23 years he was imprisoned. How did he become an iconic figure for the anti-*apartheid* movement when no-one even knew what he looked like any more?

Professor Lodge believes that it was the support of young people around the world who created an almost mythical hero. Certainly, the major rock concert held in 1988 in front of a packed Wembley stadium and a demo that demanded Mandela's release attended by 250,000 in London's Hyde Park reinforced him as an inspirational figure who should lead a new, decent South Africa. The world's youth made the song 'Free Nelson Mandela' the hottest single of the year.

Men, women and children lost their lives in this struggle. There were terrible deaths – from torture, shootings, executions. The black backlash was no less cruel. The 'necklace' of a flaming tyre became the weapon of choice in some of South Africa's poorest and most oppressed townships.

But on February 11th, 1990, Nelson Mandela was freed. In 1994, after much more talking, the first free elections were held in South Africa. Mandela was the country's first black president and he put truth and reconciliation processes in place to bring black and white together.

The 1994 election was, of course, the first time that Mandela had ever cast his vote in an election for his country's government, just as it was for all black citizens of South Africa. In his mind's eye, he was voting for all those who had died in the struggle or as a result of the struggle. These of course included his friend Oliver Tambo, Chris Hani, Chief Luthuli and Bram Fischer.

But he must also have thought of Solomon Mahlangu, who at 23 should have been able vote for a representative in his country's government but instead died so that others would have that privilege. He must have thought too of Hector Pieterson. Had he lived, he would have reached the age of 30 before he was entitled to put a piece of paper in a ballot box – the precious right of every person in the free world.

Instead, Hector was shot dead and prisoner 46664 was galvanised by the loss of such a young life to fight on, even from his prison cell, for the principles he had signed up to in Kilptown in 1955 – the ANC's Freedom Charter:

> We the people of South Africa, declare for all our country and the world to know that South Africa belongs to all who live in it, black and white.
> The people shall govern!
> All national groups shall have equal rights!
> The people shall share in the country's wealth!
> The land shall be shared among those who work it!
> All shall be equal before the law!
> All shall enjoy equal human rights!
> There shall be work and security!
> The doors of learning and culture shall be opened!
> There shall be houses, security and comfort!
> There shall be peace and friendship!

Bibliography

This book has been informed by:

Long Walk to Freedom, Nelson Mandela (Little, Brown and Company, London, 1994)

The State vs. Nelson Mandela: The trial that changed South Africa, Joel Joffe (One World Publications, 2007)

Mandela: A critical life, Tom Lodge (Oxford University Press, 2006)

Nelson Mandela: The early life of Rolihlahla Madiba, Jean Guiloineau (translated from the French by Joseph Rowe) (North Atlantic Books, 2002)

Media History, Media and Society Edited by Pieter J. Fourie (Juta Academic; second edition, 2010)

The love letters of Nelson Mandela – excerpted from *Higher Than Hope: The Authorized Biography of Nelson Mandela* (Fatima Meer, Ebony, 1990)

http://sahistory.org.za (South African History Online)

http://www.anc.org.za (ANC website)

http://www.freedom.co.za